W9-AHH-463

AMERICAN VERNACULAR

AMERICAN VERNACULAR

Regional Influences in Architecture and Interior Design

Jim Kemp

VIKING

A RUNNING HEADS BOOK

VIKING
Viking Penguin Inc., 40 West 23rd Street,
New York, New York 10010, U.S.A.
Penguin Books Ltd, 27 Wrights Lane, London W8 5TZ
(Publishing and Editorial) *and*
Harmondsworth, Middlesex, England
(Distribution and Warehouse)
Penguin Books Australia Ltd, Ringwood,
Victoria, Australia
Penguin Books Canada Ltd, 2801 John Street,
Markham, Ontario, Canada L3R 1B4
Penguin Books (N.Z.) Ltd, 182–190 Wairau Road,
Auckland 10, New Zealand

Copyright © Running Heads Incorporated, 1987
All rights reserved

First published in the U.S.A. in 1987 by Viking Penguin Inc.
Published simultaneously in Canada
First published in Great Britain in 1988 by Viking

Conceived and produced by Running Heads Incorporated, 42 East 23rd Street,
New York, New York 10010

Senior Editor: Jill Herbers
Art Direction: Stephanie Bart-Horvath
Photo Research: Christine A. Pullo and Joan Vos
Original artwork by Mona Mark

Library of Congress Cataloging-in-Publication Data

Kemp, Jim
American vernacular

Bibliography: p. 241
Includes index.
1. Architecture, Domestic—United States.
2. Vernacular architecture—United States.   3. Interior
architecture—United States.   4. Interior design—United
States.   I. Title.
NA7205.K46   1987   728′.0973   87-40117
ISBN 0-670-81309-5

British Library Cataloguing in Publication available

Color separations by Hong Kong Scanner Craft Company Ltd.
Printed in Hong Kong by
Leefung-Asco Printers Ltd.
Set in Americana

Without limiting the rights under
copyright reserved above, no part of this publication
may be reproduced, stored in or introduced into a
retrieval system, or transmitted, in any form or by
any means (electronic, mechanical, photocopying,
recording or otherwise), without the prior written
permission of both the copyright owner and the
above publisher of this book.

FOR
JOE A. TURNER
AND THE MEMORY OF
BILL CRAWFORD

ACKNOWLEDGMENTS

Every once in a great while, an author has the pleasure of indulging in a labor of love. For me, compiling AMERICAN VERNACULAR has been such an opportunity. Researching this book has taken me on many an armchair vacation to literally every corner of the country. It has given me an education in history—political, cultural, and economic. It has allowed me to continue learning about architecture and design, their history, their philosophy; and the men and women—some professional, many others not—who created them.

These journeys have been facilitiated by a number of people who took time out from their own work to help me. Their assistance forms a major portion of AMERICAN VERNACULAR and to them I offer a sincere thank-you. They include representatives of many historical societies: Cynthia Read Miller of the Henry Ford Museum, Dearborn, Michigan; Craig Williams, New York State Museum, Albany, New York; Elizabeth Warren and Stacy Hollander, Museum of American Folk Art, New York City; Sonia Lanham, Preservation Alliance of Louisville and Jefferson County, Missouri; Elaine Herrington, Curator, Chicago Architecture Foundation; Todd Strand, State Historical Society of North Dakota, Bismarck; Mary Lohrenz, Curator, State Historical Museum, Mississippi Department of Archives and History, Jackson; Joan Morris, Florida State Archives, Tallahassee; Hilary Toren, Minnesota Historical Society, St. Paul; Marilyn Stewart, Nebraska State Historical Society, Lincoln; Tom Morris, Kansas State Historical Society, Topeka.

Also, Elizabeth Jacox, Idaho State Historical Society, Boise; Milo Nave, Curator, Art Institute of Chicago; Axel Christiansen of Providence, Rhode Island, historian for the Jabez Howland House in Massachusetts; James Ryan, Olana State Historical Site, Hudson, New York; Susan Allen, Newport Art Museum, Rhode Island; Steven Frezen, Curator, Hans Herr House, and Johanna Brahms of the Daniel Boone House, both in Pennsylvania; Irene Roughton, Chrysler Museum, Norfolk, Virginia; Karen Peters, Mt. Vernon Ladies Association, Norfolk, Virginia; Jan Dorsey of the Office of Special Events at the University of Chicago; Art Olivas, State Archives, Santa Fe, New Mexico.

Thanks are also due to Susan Guerra of the California Department of Parks; Lorraine Stange and the Colonial Dames Society for photographs of the Louis Bolduc House in Missouri; Shireen Minvielle for photographs of Shadows-on-the-Teche; George Jones, City Representative's Office, Philadelphia, Pennsylvania; V. A. Patterson of the Manship House in Jackson, Mississippi; and Mariette Headly of Winterthur Museum in Delaware.

A number of manufacturers and their representatives offered invaluable assistance in obtaining photographs and information, including Sally Barnes, Williamsburg, Virginia; David Thibodeau, public relations representative of Willsboro Wood Products, Boston, Massachusetts; Joyce Clark and Tom McKay of Knoll International in New York City; Sarah McDonell, Shaker Workshops, Arlington, Massachusetts; Nancy Carter of Buller and Associates; Bob Grant of Grant's Furniture, Lake Placid, New York; Linda Donaldson, Lane Furniture, Altavista, Virginia; John Hagerty, Cohasset Colonials, Cohasset, Massachusetts; Robert Colleen, Kindel Furniture, Grand Rapids, Michigan; Chris Babcock, Harden Furniture Co., McConnellsville, New York; Danielle Shaw of Sotheby Parke Bernet, as well as Henry Snuggs and Judy Todd of Christie's, both in New York City.

In addition, I am personally indebted to several photographers and their associates for painstaking research and reservoir of knowledge: Norman McGrath and his assistant Bridget Leicester of New York City; James Levin, also of New York City; and James Brett of Phoenix, Arizona, an author in his own right. I am particularly thankful to two other photographers—and cherished friends—who always come through: Robert Perron of Branford, Connecticut and Peter Loppacher of New York City.

AMERICAN VERNACULAR was prepared under the auspices of Running Heads Incorporated of New York City and there is no finer group of people with whom an author can hope to work. I would also like to thank Louise Quayle, who copyedited the text with such thoroughness. The beautiful graphic design is the work of Stephanie Bart-Horvath. There would be no book if it weren't for the help of Joan Vos, who took valuable time out from her own work as an author to ferret out the lovely photographs that grace these pages. She sets the standard for photo research. Other illustrative material was gathered by Chris Pullo. I am especially indebted to Jill Harper Herbers of Running Heads, who has seen this book—and others—through more than one trauma. She is the sort of editor—and lady—with whom a writer can only hope to work. I would also like to thank Michael Fragnito and Barbara Williams of Viking, both of whom offered support and advice throughout the project.

Finally, I would like to offer my sincere appreciation for the support of Gordon Firth, Susan Boyle (who walks softly but carries a big editing pencil), Trish Foley, Richard Horn, Mindy Drucker, and Tracey Harden for generously contributing their time and their thoughts—but most of all for sharing treasured friendships.

CONTENTS

INTRODUCTION

A new spirit of adventure abounds in America—the rediscovery of tradition. It is manifested in almost every realm of American life. In the first part of the eighties, the country's political outlook grew conservative; political rhetoric began to reverberate with the language of patriotism and the glorification of "traditional family values." Interest in the American character filtered down from there and caught on, regardless of political beliefs. Everywhere, it seems, Americans are celebrating America.

A clarification of the title is in order. The term "vernacular" may be one of the most frequently used—but least understood— terms in architecture. "Vernacular architecture" can have several meanings. It can mean strictly regional house-types and styles. It can also mean a non-indigenous or foreign style that has been built with local, non-traditional materials, such as an English stone house design constructed of wood. Vernacular in both architecture and the decorative arts can also encompass artifacts that are—to use the term in vogue today—low-end. An excellent example is mass-produced kitsch from the 1930s, which represents an amalgamation and bastardization of the Art Nouveau and Art Deco styles. For this book, "vernacular" is limited to regional architectural styles and house-types, thus eliminating other bona-fide but perhaps confusing meanings of the term.

Traditionalism is also a major influence in the arts. High-style architecture is on a trajectory away from Modernism into Post-modernism, which marries functional International Style space-planning to historic decorative embellishments such as cornices and moldings. Decoration is the operative word in interior design, as is evidenced by the popularity of painted finishes, elaborate window treatments, and historically inspired furnishings.

One of the focal points of this movement back to the future is the reacquaintanceship by architects, designers, and home-owners with a long-neglected realm—regional architecture and design. Rising out of and, in a sense, embodying a particular location and cultural tradition, each of America's native housing styles—from the New England Saltbox and the New Mexico adobe to the Southeastern Dogtrot—is being enjoyed once again for its inherent beauty and practicality.

Though distinctly different, these types of houses have much in common. Each reflects its locale in terms of building methods and materials, climate control, and exterior styling. In New England, for example, houses were built with high-peaked roofs so that snow would slide easily to the ground instead of accumulating atop the structure. The massive walls of the New Mexico adobe, sometimes two feet thick, shielded families from the strong heat of the sun during the day. On cool desert nights, the walls re-radiated the solar gain indoors as space heating.

Regional architecture always has been characterized by the use of local building materials—wood in New England, stone in the Mid-Atlantic region, and, in the Midwest, where trees were scarce, the earth itself in the form of sod. The color palette, too, reflected the regional environment. A glistening coat of whitewash to reflect sunlight was usually applied as the finishing touch to the exteriors of adobe buildings in New Mexico. In the South, tin roofs served the same purpose. Red has been the exterior color of choice in New England for its ability to absorb the warmth of the sun and, thus, help heat houses through the winter.

The development of regional house-types also was governed by the size of building plots. Some of the oldest residences are farmhouses, which were the nerve centers of extensive agrarian operations. As the owners' need for space grew, farmhouses often were expanded again and again by succeeding generations, creating structures that seem to meander across the landscape. Later, as great urban centers developed, local architecture evolved to make the most of the smaller lots available to city dwellers. In Charleston, South Carolina, the response was a prototype town house called the Charleston Single. Instead of facing the street, the Charleston Single was oriented to one side of the lot to exploit the deep, narrow building sites.

In addition to houses that are stylistically associated with specific regions, American designs also include those that are indigenous to, or so closely identified with, the United States as a whole that they are considered national styles. National styles are numerous, rich in artistic sensibility, and varied in their design. The oldest classification, which is seen all across America, is Greek Revival. Classically inspired, Greek Revival was intended to imbue the young nation with a sense of history. Other national styles include the A-Frame design, which today is firmly entrenched in our minds as the archetypal lakeside or mountain retreat. The bungalow style survived transplantation from India and flourished in California, where it became a popular house model. house model.

The tradition of building to suit a particular region has been threatened, and at times overwhelmed, by outside commercial and architectural forces. Regional houses were originally built by pioneers for survival, constructed by anonymous builders forced to use the materials at hand. These early architectural examples are what architects call "vernacular" because they do not fit the progression of mainstream styles—classifications such as Georgian and Modern—by which buildings are characterized. As architectural styles changed and evolved, regional architecture was left—at least stylistically—further and further behind.

The Industrial Revolution of the 1800s spawned mass production as well as efficient systems of transportation and communication. These were serviced by a growing, inexpensive labor force, much of it consisting of poorly paid immigrants. In the building industry, these developments favored the real estate developer who could build many houses on a large tract of land and reap the economic benefits of using standardized materials and taking advantage of the economy of scale.

For their products, many developers chose some of the regional designs. However, as these house-types were adapted for the mass market, they were robbed of their most important traits, and indeed, their essence—a sense of belonging to a particular time and a specific place. Most of the time, all that remained of the original design was a general sense of exterior styling. "The 'Cape Cod Cottage' is one of those pleasant alliterations which spring readily to the lips of real estate salesmen when they are describing a small, trim, story-and-a-half house," noted a writer some fifty years ago in Building Manual, then an annual publication of House Beautiful magazine. "It is a phrase which has endured some rather loose handling. But [the style] would be a hydraheaded monster indeed if it were capable of all the disguises and odd twists which are committed in its name."

Regional furnishings suffered the same fate. Historically, the fabrication of furniture—and the establishment of style—was in the hands of the master cabinetmakers. In the nineteenth century, however, large companies assumed the control of style with their unprecedented facilities for mass production. For inspiration they turned to European designs, particularly those of France and Victorian England. When these were reinterpreted for the American mass market, many of them were contorted and watered down to the point that they became caricatures. The result was succinctly summed up by the late novelist Patrick Dennis with his descriptive play on words, "Louis le Grand Rapids."

However, these companies did produce many notable furnishings of a regional nature, albeit for national consumption. Beginning in the 1880s, a number of national companies introduced reproductions of New England Colonial furniture in varying standards of quality. In the early twentieth century, Wallace Nutting sponsored an exceptional line of colonial reproductions that have become highly prized by collectors.

At the same time, craftspersons throughout the country kept alive regional furniture-making traditions. The best known group is the Shakers, a religious order whose members produced some of the most enduring—and endearing—American designs. Because of their simple, sculptural shapes, Shaker furnishings today are prized by collectors and, thus, command high prices.

Today, regional architecture and design thrive once again. So profound is their influence that to study the subjects requires side trips into the realms of historic preservation, Modern architecture, and handicrafts. Much of the drive behind the architectural preservation movement in the United States is the direct result of a renewed appreciation for and curiosity about America's building, design, and cultural history.

The preservation of America's regional architecture is an ongoing affair. The island city of Galveston, Texas, is painstakingly rescuing its jewel-like collection of Victorian buildings lining the old main street called The Strand. Preservation groups are also active in small communities including Winchester, Virginia, where an area rich in colonial-era architecture called "Tater Hill" is in the process of being restored.

Historic preservation often is an individual endeavor. Many young adults have discovered the charm and character of regional architecture by buying and rehabilitating old structures. For some involved in these restorations, the appreciation is inherent. Others acquired their taste for the old after discovering they were priced out of the new house market.

Reproductions of regional house-types increasingly dot the landscape; many are quality, line-for-line copies of outstanding originals. Others are adaptations that may, for example, combine a Shingle-Style–inspired exterior with a modern, open floor plan in a practical, aesthetically pleasing blend of old and new.

One of the most exciting architectural developments, however, has been the incorporation of regional motifs and materials into new houses. Today, forward-thinking architects once again address the need for commonsense climate control by sensitive siting of new houses, by specifying age-old materials, and by using historic shapes. In otherwise Modern houses with flat roofs and open floor plans, it is a pleasant surprise to find regional motifs and materials. Besides adding a pleasing "humanistic" quality to the architecture, the addition of a regional sensibility alleviates the most often voiced criticisms of Modern architecture—the absence of a sense of time and place.

Postmodernists incorporate historic forms into their buildings in playful and witty ways. Architects of this persuasion take these forms—some American, some not—as a starting point, then literally "twist" them by over-scaling or rendering them in unexpected materials. The result is often visually compelling and artful.

Similar excitement for re-rendering old forms prevails in the field of interior design. Avant-garde furniture designers follow the same path as Postmodern architects by adding historic embellishments to contemporary pieces in interesting ways. Manufacturers cull the past looking for inspiration for new product lines—furniture, wall and floor coverings, ceramics, upholstery fabrics, dinnerware, and accessories.

Craftsmen and women are causing excitement of their own by keeping alive the regional furniture-making techniques and designs of the past. New reproductions made by using the original techniques are available through many craftpersons.

AMERICAN VERNACULAR celebrates the spirit—and renewed appreciation—of America's native architecture and furnishings. Organized by region, the chapters that follow explain the climate and materials, the people, and the cultural milieu that shaped the architecture and furnishings of each area. The first portion of the book is devoted to design and architecture. It illustrates the original regional building styles as well as carefully crafted reproductions, new interpretations, and, in some cases, unabashedly contemporary houses that exemplify an historically regional approach in terms of design or materials. The second portion of the

book covers regional furnishings, including furniture, textiles, ceramics, glass, metalwork, and accessories. It, too, presents original objects along with new versions.

In addition, AMERICAN VERNACULAR includes a section of indoor and outdoor details that give regional houses much of their charm and character. At the back of the book is a comprehensive list of architects, designers, manufacturers, and retailers, all of whom have a particular interest in regional architecture and furnishings. For source information on many of the architectural and design styles illustrated, consult the bibliography.

Throughout, the book showcases the old and the new, the familiar and the different. But most of all, AMERICAN VERNACULAR is a celebration of the splendid variety of architecture and design to be found in this country.

DESIGN AND ARCHITECTURE

PART I

CHAPTER ONE

Until the Industrial Revolution in the nineteenth century, houses inherently reflected their locale. However, with the rise of a new middle class and mass production, the affluent could import European architectural styles, some of which depended on materials unavailable locally to achieve the desired exterior styling. Today, architects who embrace the International Style have ignored materials historically associated with a specific place. Instead, their preference has been for materials inspired by industry—steel for structural skeletons and glass for curtain walls.

Besides indigenous materials, architecture in the twentieth century has lost other vital underpinnings that once linked it with the surroundings. Early Americans, for example, were forced to adapt a house design to the requirements of site. The development of earth-moving equipment enabled a site to be tailored for the mass construction of specific house styles. In addition, the development of mechanical air-conditioning and heating systems made it unnecessary to take advantage of local climatic conditions. To varying degrees, these twentieth-century attitudes reveal an adversarial approach to the traditional elements of architecture—siting, climate, and materials. As Sibyl Moholy-Nagy noted in her 1957 book, *Native Genius in Anonymous Architecture,* those who implement the techniques of eighteenth- and nineteenth-century builders "calculate weather and time as building aids. . . . The blazing sun dries the adobe wall. . . . The aging of wood stops warping, and the absorption and evaporation of moisture make wood roofs 'breathe' with the rhythm of the weather."

Today, many architects are rediscovering the practicality and satisfaction of working with natural building elements—the landscape, climate, and indigenous materials. Original American designs can be understood by identifying how these elements dictated construction methods of each type of house.

This cottage was remodeled along Shingle-Style lines.

SITING

A modern adobe house integrates with the Southwest landscape.

The single biggest influence on a building is its site. Early Americans coordinated the unique characteristics of a particular plot to create a family settlement suitable for sustaining life and a livelihood. Unable to alter the landscape with bulldozers, these men and women were forced to make the best of what they had. Often they had no alternative but to take the shortcomings of a site and turn them into assets.

For example, British Crown land grants were subdivided into small plots in New England. The small acreage belonging to individual families encouraged the clustering of farms. At first, this approach to siting was reinforced by a need for mutual protection. Later, it received added impetus as farmers turned to trading and crafts to supplement their meager existence from tilling the land. Families gathering in small villages tended to build houses that were stylistically similar, creating a discernible style.

Settlers in the West, on the other hand, profited from the federal government's policy of selling off huge tracts of land. As a result, owners amassed holdings in the hundreds or thousands of acres. Isolated on huge estates, the ranchers of the West built their houses to fit the lay of the land, such as nestling the house at the bottom of a ridge of foothills that served as a windbreak. Without nearby houses to emulate, Western houses assumed ruggedly individualistic characteristics ranging from sprawling

ranch houses to structures with false fronts. It is in the West that we see some of the most dramatic and creative applications of siting buildings. Lacking money, early settlers built simple structures that relied on the landscape to transcend their often undistinguished design and to create dramatic visual impact. Few buildings anywhere can equal the austere siting of a country church on a rise surrounded by miles of flat farm land. By using the grandeur of the surrounding landscape, an otherwise mundane structure is imbued with a presence that is unmatched by the most architecturally imposing cathedral.

The consolidation of landholdings into vast estates also left its mark on the regional architecture of the South. The large plantation houses of the Deep South functioned, in essence, as self-sustaining communities with a very real hierarchy—from the land owner and his family at the very top of the pyramid down to the house slaves, and, on the bottom rung, the slaves who toiled in the fields and made the entire plantation lifestyle possible.

The architecture, which echoed the role of the great English country houses as the visible seats of power of the gentry, focused on the great house of the landowner and slaveowner. The main house was serviced by a community of outbuildings housing the kitchen and slave quarters as well as barns for livestock and storage of crops.

The smaller building plots available in cities in both the North and South dictated a radically different approach to blending structure and site. In New York City, brownstones and later, apartment houses, were attached to the adjacent buildings. To encourage light and fresh air to flow into the interior, these structures opened both onto the street and to the rear. Instead of a dark interior stairwell, many small apartment buildings boasted a veranda that spanned the entire width of the building. Besides moving the stairway to the exterior, thus freeing interior space for living quarters, the veranda expanded usable space in warm weather and shielded the interior from winter snow. All year, residents could enjoy their small front gardens and lawns.

Every available plot was a potential building site in cities and towns. On narrow lots in the South, one answer was the Shotgun house, a design consisting of a string of rooms running from front to back. To save space, hallways were eliminated and each room opened directly into the next. The configuration of rooms inspired the term "Shotgun" because, the reasoning goes, a person could shoot a shotgun shell directly through the entire house without hitting a single wall. On steeply sloping city sites, builders fabricated foundations that rise in a steplike fashion gradually leading visitors up and back from the street to the entry.

These historic siting techniques are again in vogue. Architects have adapted the New England approach by planning "cluster" housing projects. Urban builders use the principle of the Charleston Single with town house and zero-lot line construction. Developers have learned that building around the contours of the landscape improves aesthetics while lowering construction costs.

CLIMATE

Before the days of mechanical heating and cooling, Americans were much more in tune with nature. This sensitivity is reflected in old buildings that were built to catch summer breezes, shelter the interior from rain and snow, and reduce the intrusion of cold. Heat, cold, rain, and snow governed the form of many older designs and, thus, gave them a special regional character.

COLD

Early Americans had to work hard to stay warm. New England Colonial houses often consisted of one room with a large, generously proportioned fireplace—often high enough to stand up in—that doubled as both a space heater and a cookstove. However, this fireplace could not supply sufficient heat for most houses so colonists placed a bench along a side wall inside the fireplace where they could sit as close as possible to the fire.

Architectural strategies also helped ward off cold. Windows were oriented to the south or west to usher solar warmth and light indoors; colder, north walls, on the other hand, were almost windowless. The Saltbox form illustrates how early American architecture adapted to the reality of the harsh winters. The distinctive long roof reaching almost to the ground on the north side of the house was a commonsense attempt to deflect the wind; the southern exposure was built with a shorter roof that allowed sunlight to pour into the house and warm the interior.

Pioneers in the West fended off the cold by adapting a Scandinavian innovation—the grass roof—to insulate their houses. When clearing the site for a simple log structure, they left a few tall pine trees in place. Over time, needles falling from the trees onto the roof created a sod base that facilitated a thick growth of grass. This "rooftop lawn," which the pioneers called *pine-to-pine,* also protected the pine roof itself from deterioration.

Another strategy designed to keep houses warm was the separate foyer, which frequently was built in houses in the 1800s. Besides creating a formal entry, the foyer provided a second interior doorway. Thus, the outside door could be opened while the interior door remained closed, preventing the loss of heat.

Today, the principles embodied in these age-old methods of staying warm are being restated within a contemporary framework. Large as they were, colonial-era fireplaces were woefully inefficient, sending most of their heat up the flue. In recent years, the fireplace has been radically redesigned, greatly increasing its usefulness. Contemporary heat-circulating fireplaces, as they are called, are equipped with fans that blow the warmth generated by burning logs through vents into the living space. In addition, the fireplace opening is fitted with glass doors to keep interior heat from escaping up the chimney.

Thanks to quantum leaps in technology, the technique of building adobe houses with thick walls to keep out unwanted cold and heat has been translated into a contemporary and nearly universal material—insulation. The protection once supplied by whitewash against assault by rain and snow can now be ordered in polyethylene sheets that are shaped into "vapor barriers" placed between exterior and interior walls. Contemporary sunrooms are built on the south or west wall of many houses to harvest solar warmth. Yesteryear's foyer has been restated as today's air-lock entry and is a staple in energy-efficient architecture.

HEAT

Porches on old Southern mansions allowed open windows for ventilation.

Heat is a given in the South and Southwest. As a friend once said, "I've been to the Sahara Desert, and it wasn't as hot as Dallas!" Heat can only be coped with, and pioneer settlers coped remarkably well. Older houses in the Deep South use a variety of cooling methods. Wide, covered porches called verandas, or galleries, wrapped completely around the Louisiana Plantation house shielding the windows and interior from direct sun. The verandas also served as auxiliary living spaces where family members could sit in the breeze and get relief from the unrelenting humidity. Second-floor balconies allowed the cooler night breeze to enter the rooms through over-scaled windows stretching from floor to ceiling to maximize airflow and ventilation.

In Texas and other Southern states, houses usually included

Architect Robert Ford designed his new passive-solar house to include an age-old Southern comfort—a belvedere. Set on the roof, the belvedere incorporates window sides that open to release hot air from the interior of the house. This particular belvedere was inspired by the one atop the Waverly Plantation, opposite.

and be exhausted outdoors. Conversely, the windows are closed in winter to keep heat indoors.

Inspired by a local plantation house named Waverly, architect Robert Ford designed a contemporary belvedere for his own new house. Ford, a member of the faculty of the School of Architecture at Mississippi State University, incorporated modern lines into an old-fashioned functional design. Like its prototype, the belvedere Ford designed is set in the center of the house to evenly ventilate all living areas in the open-plan interior and softly filter daylight into the core of the house.

Houses in the Southwest also reflect the region's particular concern with heat. Thick adobe-brick walls insulate interior living spaces by absorbing heat during the day. At night, the walls re-radiate the heat indoors to warm the interior. In addition, entry-ways are shaded by canopies formed by branches set across timbers in a rustic latticework pattern.

RAIN AND SNOW

Critical to the proper interplay between house and climate is the ability of the design to accommodate precipitation. The greatest dangers presented by precipitation are rain seepage and the weight of snow. Overlapping clapboards shed rain and made the structures of New England tight to the wind. The unique roof structure of the Saltbox also helped keep heavy snow off the roof (see pages 38–39).

In the Mid-Atlantic states, the roofs of many regional house were steeply pitched, enabling snow to fall readily to the ground. The houses built by German immigrants in Pennsylvania were constructed of stone to keep rain at bay. Like the roofs in Germany, these new American versions had second-floor dormers, which made space for an extra room and increased the amount of daylight penetrating the interior. Unlike their European proto-types, however, these dormers were fitted with an overhang to prevent rain from entering the room. To protect fireplaces from rain and snow, the chimneys were fitted with shingle roofs.

Because Louisiana receives the highest annual rainfall of any state in the nation, vernacular houses were raised off the ground, usually on an open foundation without a basement or cellar. The veranda that shaded the interior from direct sun also protected it from rain so that the windows could remain open for ventilation during heavy thunderstorms.

The extreme amount of annual snowfall in the Rocky Moun-tains prompted early settlers to construct buildings with barrel-vault cement roofs. These were finished to an absolute smooth-ness so that snow fell to the ground unimpeded. The heavy roof was supported by stone walls, which resulted in exceptionally tight construction that kept the indoors dry even if the entire structure was enveloped by snow.

In the nineteenth century, belvederes such as this one at the Waverly Plantation in Mississippi cooled Southern houses in summer.

a well-ventilated "sleeping porch" on the rear elevation. Exposed to the outdoors on three sides, the porch was open to the breeze yet protected from insects by fine mesh screens. In larger houses, the sleeping porch was located on the second floor above the trees that otherwise would hinder the airflow.

Many Southern plantation houses have belvederes atop the roof with operable windows that can be opened in warm weather. These openings create what has become known today as a "thermal chimney," which allows heat to rise through the interior

MATERIALS

Traditional materials—especially wood, stone, and masonry from local sources—remind us of a past time when such materials could not be easily transported across the country or from another continent. As Joseph Giovannini points out in the *New York Times Magazine*, building with indigenous materials captures "the spirit of place that gives buildings a feeling and meaning, and helps establish their whereabouts." For example, early builders—and their like-minded modern counterparts—selected lumber because there was a forest in the vicinity or chose stone because there was a quarry nearby.

Tough and durable, these materials were given a sense of humanity as they were manipulated by artisans. Masons created a "signature" style by arranging the stones of a wall they were building in a unique—and highly personal—way. The distinctive fanlike arrangement of cobblestones in many Southern cities represent the reach of the individual worker's arm.

WOOD

A time of hardship, the Colonial era was also a time of fine craftsmanship, as this exquisitely carved paneling amply demonstrates.

Wood is probably the most common building material, and one of the most versatile. In its humblest form, it is hacked into crude shingles to clad simple cottages. At its most sophisticated, it is crafted into finely grained paneling to give a room a sense of warmth. Wood is strong, forming the beams and joists that support multistoried structures. But when carved to form Acanthus leaves on Greek Revival columns, it is extremely delicate.

Atlantic white cedar brings to mind the houses of New England that shine like lighthouse beacons strung along the Eastern Seaboard. On America's Western shore, the great redwood forests of California are home to one of the most durable of building woods. Native—and exclusive—to the state, redwood is specified for outdoor building elements such as decks and stairways that must withstand extreme fluctuations of climate, from intense sun to torrents of rain. The Colorado vacation houses of the affluent often are constructed of simple board-and-batten, while logs form the structural heart of houses native to the Pacific Northwest. In Louisiana, where humidity levels are high all year long, the frequent choice is cypress. An almost indestructible wood highly resistant to water rot, cypress was fabricated into sewer pipes that served New York City for 200 years.

MASONRY

In older portions of the country, stonework abounds in an astonishing array of applications and quality. The first settlers in Connecticut laboriously hand-cleared the rocky land created during the glacial age. These stones were fashioned into visually striking walls that still define property boundaries. The Germans who immigrated to Pennsylvania brought with them a long history of masonry, dating back to the Roman Empire. As a result, some of the finest stone houses in America are found in Pennsylvania towns that have been bypassed by interstate highways. Local stones—often blended with brickwork—were used to build garden walls, walkways, and outdoor arches in Charleston, South Carolina.

With a seemingly boundless supply of mud in their below-sealevel homeland, the Dutch became proficient at making brick. For example, their barns have brick end-walls in which the masonry has been laid in open lacework patterns. Besides being the first "air-conditioning" in America, the open brickwork enabled an even flow of air through the interior to prevent crops from spoiling. And, because the lacework openings were small-scaled, they kept out rain while permitting light to enter. Sometimes, these new American settlers applied colorful glazing to bricks for their Dutch ovens, enhancing their ability to retain heat.

Lacking plasterboard, early builders left stone walls unfinished indoors. Today many houses, particularly those in California, are enlivened inside with a single stone wall. Besides relieving the uninterrupted expanse of smooth, monochromatic walls,

Simple brick was artfully arranged in Charleston, S.C., to make enticing walkways, walls, and hidden niches in gardens that age has made even more beautiful.

In the West, where lumber was often at a premium, nineteenth-century settlers often had no choice but to build their houses from soil.

Despite its bunkerlike connotations, masonry can be fashioned into sculptural houses that are then washed with soft pastel colors.

interior stonework adds warmth and a welcome sense of strength and permanence. To prevent the masonry from overpowering the rooms visually, it is often enlivened with windows or doorways and juxtaposed with sloped ceilings and skylights.

Stucco traditionally has been used as a finishing coat for masonry in several regions of the country. It protects the adobe bricks from damaging rain in New Mexico. In Florida, stucco conceals the unattractive concrete blocks that are *the* regional building material; one of the few that can withstand the humidity, heat, and destructive insects inherent in that environment. Stucco is often used as the finishing touch for bungalows in California. There, it has proven to be an excellent canvas for Postmodernists, who brush it with pale pastels that change in intensity and hue as the light changes throughout the day.

SOIL

Because early Americans had no choice but to build with the materials at hand, they often turned to one of the most plentiful—the earth itself. As a result, soil was used in a number of ingenious ways. Soil became the filler between the timbers in early log houses in many portions of the country. In the Midwest, where wood was scarce, soil was placed on rooftops to insulate the interior from summer heat and winter cold. Sometimes, an entire house was made of sod. The most primitive sod houses resemble a large mound punctuated by a stovepipe. More elaborate examples are completely above-ground and have framed-in windows. Today, earth-sheltering is being revived, albeit in a vastly different form. In many parts of the Midwest, houses are designed with mounds of soil along the exterior walls. These earth berms, as they are called, retain winter coolness far into the warm season and hold in summer heat during the winter.

GLASS

Glass is so firmly associated with International-Style buildings that we tend to forget that it is an ancient building material. Almost everyone is familiar with the beautiful stained glass in Medieval cathedrals, but fewer know that glass was also prominent in much less exuberant motifs in Tudor houses where many tiny diamond-shaped pieces were combined to form large windows.

In America, small pieces of half-moon glass were placed above the front door of New England farmhouses to illuminate the interior during the day. In a number of architectural styles—especially rural ones—larger panes or transoms were set above interior doors, allowing light to flow from the rooms into a central hallway. By placing the glass in a hinged frame, owners could open the transom in the summer for ventilation.

Contemporary architects often weave glass into regionally inspired structures in clever and practical ways. Open air courtyards in places as diverse as New York City and Houston have been enclosed with huge glass skylights. This approach lets in sun as the skylight protects the courtyard from precipitation, promoting year-round use. Architects who use solar design in their houses often specify a glass-enclosed sunroom or solarium to collect heat. The glass also frames and brings indoors landscape views that make the interior seem much larger.

The use of glass has been greatly facilitated by the development of double- and triple-pane glazing. Far superior for insulating a house than the single-pane variety, double- and triple-pane glazing are commonly specified for houses built in northern and Alpine climates to help keep heat from escaping outdoors without reducing the amount of sunlight penetrating the interior.

METAL

The Shakers were masters at making highly detailed metal hardware.

In colonial America, iron was forged into crude stakes to bind timbers together. In the eighteenth and nineteenth centuries, craftsmen handwrought common metals into delicate hardware accessories including door hinges, pulls, and latches. Along the Eastern Seaboard, finer metals such as brass were forged into trivets to protect fragile tabletops.

One of the most distinctive applications of metal, however, was in construction. Throughout the South and New England, houses were topped with tin roofs. In the South, the tin reflected sunlight to prevent the structure from absorbing heat. In New England, they acted as a "slide" so that heavy winter snows would slip to the ground instead of accumulating on the roof, where its weight could cause structural damage. Because of its practical uses for different climates, the metal roof is still prevalent throughout both of these regions.

TILE

Large tiles become a practical, lovely floor in a California house.

Throughout the Southwest and West, houses designed and built around a regional theme reflect the powerful design influence of Spain and Mexico by incorporating extensive amounts of tile. For example, houses in the Spanish Mediterranean style native to South Texas have roofs of curved tiles and walls of stucco or brick. In California, Mexican ceramic tile also is used outdoors for patios and walkways. Indoors, it is specified as a floor treatment to add a sense of visual warmth in rooms with large areas of glass.

Though tile has always been a common building material in these regions, it became even more popular in the years following the 1973 Arab oil embargo. The draconian reduction in the amount of oil imported into the United States—and the ensuing price hikes—prompted many Americans to turn to an ancient method of heating: passive-solar sunrooms and solariums. Some were added onto existing houses; others were included in new residential designs. To camouflage the thick, unsightly concrete floor required to store solar heat, architects and designers called for a decorative floor treatment of ceramic or Mexican tile.

COLOR

Red paint establishes the New England location of this old barn.

All too often, we forget the enormous importance of color in architecture and interior design. It establishes a mood, defines spaces in modern, open-plan houses, and accents architectural details. For much of the twentieth century, however, color has been ignored, probably because Modernism, the dominant architectural style of our time, eschewed color—bright or pale—in favor of white.

Today we are seeing a renewed emphasis on color. The palette of Postmodern architects and designers is pale and subtle. Other designers have embraced the colors of fashion, which now are deep saturated blacks and reds as well as rich pastels—turquoise, pink, and yellow—that have been publicized by television shows such as *Miami Vice*.

Regionally inspired colors remain a force in contemporary architecture, though distinctions have been considerably blurred by the mass production and distribution of national paint brands. The earliest English colonists were not at all concerned with color. Their interest was in survival. As a result, their houses usually were left unpainted—inside and out—with only an occasional piece of painted furniture to inject a welcome spot of color.

In the eighteenth century, when survival was assured, another concern emerged—style. Settlers brought to America the color preferences of their mother countries, which were combined with the colors and climate of their new homeland. For example, later colonists preferred the colors popular in England including buff, gray-green, cream, and brown.

Other colors were inspired by nature. One of the most popular in New England—then and now—is red, which was applied on the exteriors of barns and houses to help absorb solar heat. In the days before paint was manufactured, New Englanders created a mixture of rust (scraped from nails and fences), skim milk, and lime that coated the wood like a varnish. Many new houses in the region, which otherwise reflect no regional influences, are painted red to blend in with their older neighbors.

Red was also used indoors to evoke a feeling of warmth during the cold winter. Sometimes the color red occurred naturally as the unfinished plank pine boards aged.

In the South, where staying cool was a prime concern, light colors were chosen to reflect sunlight and prevent heat buildup indoors. White was particularly popular and remains so today for both its climatic influence and to imbue the old plantation houses with a sense of grandeur, permanancy, and authority.

White was also favored in the Southwest for the adobe houses that annually were coated with whitewash. Though this tradition continues today, the choice is often a beige that blends the structure with its landscape. Sometimes, white and beige are combined within a single house, suggesting Postmodern overtones.

Other areas are noted for their unique colorways. Charleston, South Carolina, for example, is noted for its distinctive, local palette of pale pastels—pinks and yellows in particular—offset by white trim. Just as unique are the vibrant colors that grace San

Pink is one of the most famous of Charleston's regional colors.

Francisco's Victorian houses—"the painted ladies"—and remind us of the city's *recherché* past.

The interest in selecting colors that are inspired by a geographical region or a specific architectural style has prompted paint manufacturers to offer them as part of their product lines. One of the most successful of these is the "Cape May" collection by Fuller-O'Brien. The assortment of color paints offered by this company reflects the color palette associated with the New Jersey resort, which has one of the largest concentrations of restored Victorian houses in the country.

HISTORIC ROOF SHAPES

GABLE

The gable roof tops a number of American housing styles, from the Cape Cod cottage to the New England farmhouse to the Colonial house. In the case of the Cape Cod cottage, shown here, the roof was punctuated by dormer windows that extended living space for a second floor. During the nineteenth century, it was flattened out to top the Greek Revival style house. Today, the gable roof is often replicated exactly as it was utilized in the Colonial era. Far more interesting are contemporary adaptations in which the roof is greatly overscale, set at an extremely sharp pitch, and even cut into to form a curve.

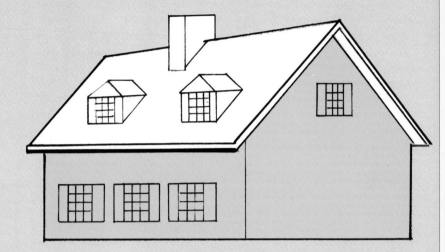

SALTBOX

The gable roof was extended on one side with the addition of a lean-to to form the distinctive Saltbox silhouette. Particularly popular—and practical—in New England, the Saltbox was sited so that the long side faced north. This enabled the long side to deflect bitter winter winds while the short side looked south allowing direct sunlight to enter both floors and warm the interior.

LEAN▪TO

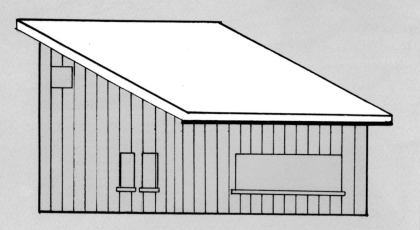

The lean-to was an efficient method of expand-ing living space at little expense. The first lean-tos were attached to the rear of the house. Be-cause the roof of the lean-to was not integrated with the existing structure, it stood out as an ob-vious addition. As the lean-to became used more frequently on new houses, the roofline gradually was blended into the overall architecture as in the case of the Saltbox.

GAMBREL

Associated with barn construction, the gambrel roof is distinguished by its sides, which have two slopes, the lower slopes being the steeper. The gambrel roof often tops what is today called Dutch Colonial architecture.

HIP

French colonists brought their own distinctive roof to the New World—the hip roof. Unlike other roof forms, the hip roof not only has sloping sides, it also has sloping ends. Frequently the four sides are of equal dimensions, creating a square house. In addition, the hip roof often ex-tends out as a deep eave held in place by vertical supports that create plenty of shade.

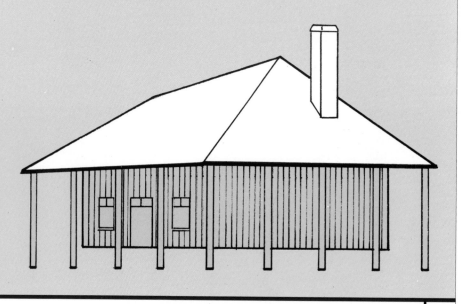

A PORTFOLIO OF REGIONAL STYLES

PART

II

CHAPTER

TWO ■

Probably no single region of the country has a wider variety—and a more thoroughly documented—range of house-types and architectural styles than New England. From the rustic historicism of the Cape Cod Cottage to the city air of the New York town house, New England shows a wide diversity of styles. The breadth is so great, in fact, that the houses of New England create a veritable patchwork of architectural and cultural history of the United States—from its Pilgrim-era infancy through today.

This lovely house bears all the earmarks of the eighteenth-century New England farmhouse even down to its broad façade and classical pediment fashioned from wood. The lean-to, which is placed at the side, is a later—yet harmonious—addition.

CAPE COD COTTAGE

As old as America itself, the historic Cape Cod Cottage can be traced directly back to the Pilgrims. Literally a definition of architectural simplicity, the prototype Cape Cod Cottage was a small, one-and-a-half story, gable-roofed structure with the front door and fireplace located at one end of the house. The spartan front door was made of planks in early versions, and the exterior walls were clad with clapboard or shingles that were left unpainted to weather to a pleasing gray in the salt air.

A variety of the Cape Cod Cottage, but not nearly as popular, was the Cape Ann Cottage. It was designed and built the same as the Cape Cod except for the roof, which was a gambrel design.

An eminently functional design, the full Cape Cod Cottage-style house has a center doorway on the first floor and dormer windows upstairs that increase living space.

A restrained selection of antique furnishings emphasizes the moldings and other millwork inside this beautifully restored Cape Cod Cottage.

A chair rail protects furnishings and guides the eye laterally across the room making the small rooms in a Cape Cod Cottage seem bigger.

The Cape Cod Cottage may well be America's first modular house. The tiny, basic house was called the "Honeymoon," or "half," cottage. As a family grew, the basic box house was expanded with an addition placed at the end nearest the entry. This first small addition created a "three-quarter" Cape, which is the most common type of Cape Cod Cottage found today. For more living space, this end of the house was expanded a second time, resulting in the "full," or "double," Cape with the front door now located in the center of the façade.

Original half-Cape cottages are tiny, consisting of a single room on the first floor. Yet even the full-Cape has only two ground-floor rooms. To increase the size of the rooms on the second floor of some Capes, the upper floor was expanded by building dormer windows. These were protected from the weather by small gable roofs.

To meet today's radically greater need for living space, many original Cape Cod Cottages have been artfully expanded. For example, a contemporary addition might be placed against the rear wall to create more interior space while preserving the original architectural lines and charm of the house when viewed from the street. To reinforce the aura of period authenticity, the addition can be made from an old structure such as a barn or even part

The traditional form and materials of the Cape Cod Cottage have been artfully restated in a contemporary vein by architect Christopher Woerner.

In this delightful, contemporary adaptation of the Cape Cod Cottage style, architect Grattan Gill eschewed the traditional second-floor dormer windows for a clerestory. Designed so that it faces south, the clerestory brings natural sunlight into the center of the structure.

of another house. This sort of expansion is an excellent strategy for adding a contemporary kitchen that complements rather than dilutes the original architecture.

The Cape Cod Cottage is probably the single most copied house form in America, from tract houses in 1950s subdivisions to manufactured structures that are shipped and constructed on-site. While many of these merely echo the general form, others are striking renditions. The Cape Cod Cottage has also served as an inspiration for unmistakably contemporary houses. The new versions rely on the traditional silhouette of the house-form as well as on the authentic materials, usually gray shingles. From that point, however, the architecture departs significantly from the original cottage. For example, one wall might be extended to create a light-filled bay and the roof fashioned into an overhang that shelters an outdoor deck. Generally, these new houses also incorporate much greater glazing than their stylistic ancestors for higher levels of natural illumination. Sometimes, large windows are supplemented with modern greenhouses. In almost all cases, the house is designed with outdoor decks to capture scenic views and expand usable living space.

Indoors, these houses are contemporary, in keeping with modern space-planning tenets. These may include open planning, two-story-high living rooms, and modern kitchen design.

The low-slung, trim silhouette of the house changes radically when viewed from the opposite side. Here, the traditional Cape Cod Cottage influences give way to an unabashedly contemporary spirit.

On the lower floor of the south wall is a string of greenhouse extensions. Besides economically expanding living space, these bays harvest direct-gain solar warmth that lowers winter heating bills.

COLONIAL

Part of an old barn was recycled by The 18th Century Company to become a modern kitchen in a Colonial house in Connecticut. The charm and graciousness of the old materials belie the very practical, contemporary space-planning used in the kitchen.

As settlers moved from the Atlantic coastline further into the interior of New England, they adapted the basic Cape Cod Cottage to meet the new environment. The result of this evolution was the New England Colonial house, which remains one of the oldest and most popular forms of American residential architecture.

Authentic New England Colonial houses vary considerably, from the rustic to the exceedingly sleek. Generally, examples of the New England Colonial style share several architectural characteristics: a square or rectangular shape with a wing extending from the rear or one side; a shingled, gable roof; fireplaces at each end; an elaborate cornice with dentils; and traditional oak structural beams and clapboard siding.

The New England Colonial and other early house-types were built by using the technique of timber-frame construction. In fact, timber-framing is the single most identifying characteristic of early English and English-influenced construction.

Early in the nineteenth century, timber-framing died out with the development of water-powered sawmills and the subsequent introduction of stud-framing. Today, timber-framing has been revived because of its inherent structural stability and the air of authenticity that it lends houses imbued with traditional styling.

The contemporary method of timber-framing is to cut the structural beams at a factory and then join them on-site. The beams are assembled with pegs called trunnels, or tree nails, creating the distinctive traditional wood joinery. Timber-framing is used today by a small but influential number of craftspeople such as Tedd Benson of Alstead, New Hampshire, and The 18th Century Company of Durham, Connecticut.

The New England Colonial form has been revived again and again. The first wave of reproductions, inspired by the American Centennial celebration, were built in the 1870s. In the 1930s, speculative builders adapted many historic American architectural forms for mass-market consumption, no doubt to make developments more acceptable to buyers by employing familiar shapes. Though criticized for their often free-form interpretation of the historic shape, many of these houses offer the advantages of beautiful materials and solid construction. They have aged so that they no longer stand out starkly as "new" antiques and are often charming. Colonial-inspired decorative treatments further imbue these houses with the aura of the eighteenth century.

Reproductions of the New England Colonial house continue to be built today. Like their 1930s counterparts, these new houses reflect the era of their construction as much as they do the historic prototype. For example, many families are asking architects to design custom Colonial-style houses that are unmistakably upscale in their appearance and amenities—from dramatic (though inauthentic) Palladian-inspired curved windows to whirlpool baths and exercise rooms.

Some architects and builders go to great lengths to achieve a sense of authenticity. This is best achieved by specifying contemporary elements that reflect the aura of the old: old-looking yet modern 12-over-12 windows, red cedar siding turned inside out to achieve the look of clapboard, and a fireplace that is copied from an historic design.

New materials form a contemporary version of the traditional Colonial fireplace.

SALTBOX

The most distinctive characteristic of the Saltbox house is its roof, which is shorter on the south-facing side. With this approach, sunlight is encouraged to enter both levels of the house to warm the interior on cold winter days. The exterior is clad with clapboard siding.

Though the New England Saltbox is thought of as a quintessentially American design, it was actually imported from England by the early colonists. The Saltbox developed during the Tudor era when the traditional, one-room deep English cottage was enlarged with a lean-to at the rear to add extra living space. This change created the distinctive asymmetric gable roof, which is short on one side of the house and long on the other.

The first Saltbox houses in the New World were essentially one-and-a-half or two-story structures with one room on each floor and the fireplace and front door at one end.

The Saltbox has much in common with the Cape Cod Cottage. Both were clad with clapboard or shingles. They both also were expanded with the addition of a section immediately beyond the chimney and front door. From there, however, the Saltbox took a different developmental route. Instead of being expanded further to the side like the Cape Cod Cottage, the Saltbox was enlarged with the addition of a lean-to shed that spanned the entire rear wall. This made the mature form of the Saltbox two rooms deep with a massive chimney directly in the center of the house.

A modern Saltbox carefully preserves the distinctive roof configuration and clapboard siding of the original shown on the opposite page.

The interior of this Saltbox house reflects its Colonial origins in the large masonry fireplace. Exposed beams and timbers and a traditional decorating scheme featuring a wing chair and historic accessories enhance the ambience of a bygone time preferred by many Americans.

The short-roofed façade was oriented to the south so that it faced the sun and took advantage of its warmth in winter. On the front and sides were large double-hung windows to maximize solar gain. In Tudor fashion, they consisted of numerous small panes, generally twelve panes to each sash. The low-sloping roof on the opposite side faced north where it deflected winter winds.

Though generally considered a New England regional house-type, a few Saltboxes were constructed in the South. There, the type was called a Catslide.

The Saltbox readily lends itself to creative remodeling. Because of its practicality and historic charm, the Saltbox also is the most widely reproduced antique house form in America next to the Cape Cod Cottage. Many of these houses are remarkable for their fidelity to the original design. For example, the façade on a contemporary Saltbox by architect William M. Thompson is an exact replica of the prototype. Classic, too, are the building materials including the 4-inch-wide clapboards for the exterior cladding. To reflect a contemporary spirit, however, the side elevation departs from the original shape by incorporating a wing that greatly expands living space.

NANTUCKET COTTAGE

The Nantucket Cottage has been faithfully re-created by Timberpeg, Inc., as a kit house.

These tiny structures, which served as the headquarters for whalers, were familiar sights along the Atlantic coastline in the seventeenth and eighteenth centuries. Though this way of life disappeared long ago, the distinctive regional house-type remains. Original, seventeenth-century Nantucket Cottages were built with the fireplace and entry located at one end. The interior consisted of one room that soared to the peak of the ceiling. The end of the room by the hearth and entry door was reserved for

cooking; the opposite end was used as a sleeping area.

To accommodate families' greater need for comfortable sleeping space, the cottages were enlarged with lean-tos placed on the front or rear wall and, often, on both. For even more room, a raised platform was built above the sleeping area in the original portion of the cottage.

Modern interpretations of the Nantucket Cottage are loyal, for the most part, to the architectural lines and small size of the orig-

A ceiling that rises to the roofline makes the small cottage seem larger.

inal form. An exceptionally charming and faithful recreation is actually a kit house-model called "Barnhouse" manufactured by Timberpeg, Inc. Architect Lyman S.A. Perry of Newtown Square, Pennsylvania, selected this kit when he built a retreat on Nantucket Island. Though the front door is placed differently from the original cottage form, Perry notes, "The rustic materials, gabled roof, and divided windows of the 'Barnhouse' made it especially well suited to Nantucket's architectural style."

The architect took the basic kit and customized it by adding a guest house and trellised breezeway to the main two-story structure. As an individual touch, he added a curved window that brightens the second floor.

Unlike original Nantucket Cottages, the upper level of Perry's house is not an open loft area but is divided into two bedrooms and a communal bath. Even here, however, the design adheres to tradition with the ceiling following the angle of the roof.

SHINGLE STYLE

This Shingle-Style house displays the traditional influences of New England in the styling of its gambrel roof. The expansive wrap-around porch reflects the influence of the Victorian Age.

At some point in every age, architects and their clients seek design inspiration from the past. While many are content merely to copy an historic style, others "use" the past as a starting point to develop architecture that is entirely different and new. Such was the genesis of the Shingle Style, which took root along the Eastern Seaboard in the late nineteenth century.

Architect Henry Hobson Richardson built the first Shingle Style structure, the Watts-Sherman House, in 1874. He was soon followed by the firm of McKim, Mead, and White, builders of the Low

A new Shingle-Style house on Long Island designed by architect Lawrence Randolph is clad in the traditional manner but limits the sweeping gable roof associated with this house-type to the living area.

In the living area, a large curved-top window tradition gives way to sleek contemporary decorating and architectural detailing including a sloped ceiling, exposed beams, and a set of glazed French doors.

Dormer windows enliven the roof of this Shingle-Style–inspired house by Graham Gund Associates.

When architect Lawrence Randolph adapted the Shingle Style for his own house, he imbued it with classical symmetry.

House in 1887. These and other architects created airy, voluminous houses that—for the time—incorporated state-of-the-art amenities including central heating.

The inspiration for this new house-type was New England Colonial architecture. From that era, architects borrowed the basic shape and the gable roof. Greatly over-scaled, the gable roof became the single most important motif of the new style. Shingle-Style houses were built in a variety of architectural styles including Saltboxes and lean-tos. These houses also often had large wrap-

around verandas in keeping with their Victorian vintage.

As architectural historian Vincent Scully notes, the Shingle Style later gave way to builders' tract-houses of the twentieth century. However, in 1959 the publication of a book by Scully, *The Shingle Style*, revived this unusual architectural form. Like their predecessors, new Shingle-Style houses take a variety of forms. Some combine a simple cottage and an exaggerated roof to achieve a contemporary aura; others seem traditional until the viewer notices sliding glass doors and other modern elements.

FARMHOUSE

The nineteenth-century New England farmhouse was wrapped with porches in the best Victorian manner, left. A contemporary example designed by architect Ric Weinschenk soars beneath a gable roof, right.

The distinctive New England farmhouse is the chameleon of American architecture—it has kept pace with changing times by assuming the guise of whatever exterior style was in vogue. The interior, however, has managed to remain virtually unchanged.

The typical seventeenth-century New England farmhouse was a primitive, two-story structure consisting of two rooms. Downstairs was the "hall," where the family worked, cooked, and ate around the warmth of the fireplace located on one of the end walls. Above that was the sleeping space.

Many of these houses were expanded in the eighteenth century and became the farmhouse form that is most familiar today. The farmhouse grew to the side, generally along the fireplace wall so that it was located in the center of the house. In this con-

figuration, the farmhouse consisted of two rooms on the first floor: the original hall, and the new parlor, which, as the most important room of the house, was the equivalent of our living room.

Sometimes the simple box form was "turned" so that the end wall faced the street, and the entry was relocated to this new façade. Traditionally, the exterior was clad with clapboard and the roof was steeply pitched to shed snow. The chimney remained in the center of the house to offer structural support, and the layout remained the same with two square rooms on each floor. This is the form many new renditions of the New England farmhouse take today.

During the Victorian Age, the interior of the New England farmhouse remained virtually intact, although it was sometimes

This authentic New England farmhouse was in a complete state of disrepair before it was rehabilitated. Though the façade was painstakingly restored, the house was reshaped inside to conform to contemporary living patterns and spatial needs.

altered to accommodate a center hallway. The exterior merely adopted the styling motifs that were popular at the time, such as the wide porches that stretch across the façade and along the sides of farmhouses from the 1880s.

The farmhouse remains a favorite house-type in New England. Many of the originals, regardless of the date of their construction, are eagerly sought out and remodeled. An especially sensitive remodeling of a Victorian New England farmhouse was undertaken by architect Eric A. Chase, who followed the lines of the original structure when he designed a new porch.

The interior has been updated with built-in shelving in the study off the living room and a row of three windows in the bedroom. The glazing indoors overcomes the primary complaint by many owners of old houses—their excessively dark interiors.

The New England farmhouse has inspired striking contemporary versions. A case in point is a house designed by architect Ric Weinschenk in Maine. His design has a gable roof, a long façade, and a contemporary version of the traditional oval window above the entry. In this case, however, a trio of smaller gable roofs faces the street along with the covered entry that is supported by columns.

A glazed shed extension creates a perfect greenhouse for nurturing flowering plants.

An existing extension to the side was redesigned into an open-plan dining area with a view outdoors through the extension.

COLONIAL GARRISON

A frontier house-type, the Colonial Garrison was built on the edge of the settled territory to function as a defense center during attacks by unfriendly Indians. Designed as a two-story structure, the Colonial Garrison took one of two variations: either a straight façade or one with the second floor built as an overhang above the ground level.

As Mary Mix Foley points out in *The American House*, the Colonial Garrison house was only one variation of the Jettied House, so called for its protruding second story. The interior arrangement was basically that of the New England farmhouse. The first floor was divided into a hall and a parlor with bedrooms upstairs.

The Colonial Garrison style was revived and popularized by many subdivision developers in the 1960s for two reasons: the simple, rectangular shape was quick and economical to build and the design could easily be marketed as "historical."

Though the simple lines of the Colonial Garrison house bore many people, they make this house eminently suitable to remodeling. In fact, the Colonial Garrison is frequently enlarged with additions at the front or rear and, sometimes, both. The owners of a 1960s Colonial Garrison-style house in New England did just that, enlivening the façade with an extension to convert a ground-floor bedroom into a master suite containing a private bath and sitting room. Along the rear wall, a screened porch and curved deck were added to expand the outdoor entertaining area. The deck is used in spring and fall, the screened porch in summer—the bug season—when the fine mesh keeps insects outdoors.

An overhanging second floor brings Colonial Garrison overtones to this structure.

BARN

An old dilapidated barn was remodeled along contemporary lines into a home by James H. Somes, Jr. of JSA Associates.

The classic New England barn is a two- or two-and-a-half story building topped with either a gambrel or gable roof and, sometimes, a cupola. The New England barn obviously is not an historic type of housing but it does possess a distinctive vernacular style. In addition, many barns in New England have been converted into living units and have even inspired the design of new houses.

The conversion of structures never intended for housing is known as *adaptive re-use*. The transformation can be fairly straightforward, giving the converted unit the look of the old, or it can be a complete redesign of the original structure. The 18th Century Company, for example, remodeled an old barn into a house and retained the spirit of the original structure. In fact, the basic shape of the barn was kept completely intact and was altered only to accommodate an entry, windows that illuminate and ventilate the interior, and a fireplace chimney.

The emphasis on traditional design and detailing was continued indoors. In the living room, the original ceiling joists and structural beams are left exposed. The double-hung windows are in a 6-over-6 configuration rather than 12-over-12 in keeping with the scale of the structure. Though new, the random-width plank floor respects the old-time spirit of the rest of the structure.

An entirely different approach was taken by architect James

An old barn has been remodeled to neatly accommodate a modern kitchen.

H. Somes, Jr. of JSA Architects in Portsmouth, New Hampshire, who remodeled a 200-year-old barn into a year-round home for his family. This house also will serve as an inspiration for anyone who has wanted to remodel an old structure into a home but was disheartened by its deteriorated condition. When Somes purchased the barn, it was in a state of extreme disrepair. However, Somes was able to look beyond the structure's shanty ambience and see its very real possibilities as a house.

Clad with white cedar shingles treated with a bleaching oil to produce the weathered gray appearance, the exterior is a study in stylish contemporary architecture that loses none of its original barnlike profile. As an added plus, Somes kept the remodeling cost down to $25 a square foot, which is quite an achievement when compared to the square-foot cost of $60 to $100 of some projects. The project was given a merit award for remodeling and rehabilitation in recognition of its "clean, fresh, lively but faithful interpretation of the original barn."

Because old barns are usually extremely large structures, scaling the interior to human size is of primary concern. For example, the barn that Somes remodeled was twice as large as the 2800 square feet of living space his family needed. To make the interior smaller while keeping the distinctive lines of the structure,

Architect Don Hisaka of Cambridge, Mass., borrowed—and updated—the simple barn shape for a weekend retreat.

Inside, Hisaka opted for an open floor plan with a combination living, dining, and kitchen area with highly detailed woodwork made from stock materials.

open and closed decks were "carved" out of the barn. Besides shrinking the overall living area, the decks serve as transitional spaces between the outdoors and the interior.

Rather than simply copy the barn style, architect Don M. Hisaka of Cambridge, Massachusetts, used the form as a starting point to design a new house. Playful and whimsical, the house incorporates many design elements that are associated with barns: the steeply pitched gable roof and overhangs at the front and back, for example. A weathered look was achieved by applying gray stain on the shiplap cedar siding.

A pastiche of old and new, the house includes commercial-grade sliding glass doors that serve as the entry and a large square window divided into four quadrants by strips of aluminum. These contemporary elements are further enlivened by new renditions of a pergola above the entry and a belvedere-like structure on the deck that echoes the grid motif of the large window.

The exterior may be regionally inspired, but the interior is strictly contemporary. The living and dining area is arranged as one room, which makes the small house seem much larger. Sliding glass doors and a square window direct attention to the outdoor view. In addition, the sloped ceiling rises approximately twenty-two feet high, directing the viewer's eye upward. This height is emphasized by the exposed fireplace flue and ceiling rafters. A series of crossties accentuates the width of the room.

CHAPTER

THREE ∎

The architecture of the Mid-Atlantic region is rich in history. The many groups who settled in these states—New York, Pennsylvania, New Jersey, and Maryland—have created an intricate tapestry of intriguing materials and shapes. Taking advantage of stone and other native materials, these groups built practical yet handsome dwellings. The influences on the architecture of the Mid-Atlantic region are as international as the people who settled there. What makes the buildings uniquely American is the way their creators interpreted architectural styles from their native lands—Flanders, Holland, and Germany among others—into dwellings that still seduce and inspire us today.

A modern "Dutch farmhouse" by architect Robert S. Bennett incorporates a wonderful abundance of contemporary glazing.

NEW YORK CITY BROWNSTONE

Margaret Helfund's home is a classic example of the brownstone.

Anyone who has visited New York City probably has wandered through Greenwich Village, the Upper West Side, or Brooklyn Heights marveling at the rows of attached houses called brownstones. A structure that is unique to New York City, the name "brownstone" belies the materials from which it is made. In fact, there is no such thing as brownstone. Instead, the material actually is a type of sandstone that is usually reddish-brown in color.

The brownstone developed from the need for housing within the space limitations imposed by an urban setting. Lots were—and remain—extremely narrow and deep. This sort of site dictated an equally narrow, long structure. To make the most of every available inch, open space between neighboring brownstones was eliminated entirely. The restricted site also encouraged

builders to look up and construct brownstones three to five stories high. Because brownstones—and their more elegant relatives, New York City town houses—are connected to create a pleasing, unified front, both are sophisticated versions of that standby of urban working-class shelter, the rowhouse.

The brownstone originally was built for middle-class New Yorkers in the nineteenth century. Brownstones generally fell into two categories: single-family residences and small apartment houses that, as a rule, are twice as wide.

Though designed in many different architectural styles, brownstones have several elements in common. The ornate, double-door entry generally is located on the second floor and reached by an exterior staircase. Indoors, public rooms are on

The woodwork in the parlor is beautifully restored.

the second floor while bedrooms are isolated on the levels above. The kitchen is in the basement. However, hard and fast rules are deceiving as brownstone design was subject to changes in design taste. For example, many brownstones that were built on the Upper West Side of Manhattan in the 1880s and 1890s were designed in what is called the American basement plan. With this approach, the exterior staircase was eliminated and the brownstone was entered on the ground level.

Until the 1960s, brownstones were far more numerous than they are today. Many of them were demolished in the name of progress to make way for anonymous high-rise buildings. The loss was tragic for New York City, which sacrificed one of its most distinctive architectural features in the name of "urban renewal."

Because they offer spaciousness, albeit vertically, in a crowded city and can be remodeled into lovely residences, brownstones that remain are among the most avidly sought forms of housing in New York City today. Architect Margaret Helfund remodeled a splendid brownstone into a home that combines the best of the past and present. On the exterior, large windows that enabled light and air to flow from both the front and back remain intact, but are now fitted with contemporary single-sheet glazing that accentuates the architrave, or overhang, above them.

The living room is alive with ceiling detail and wide window moldings, which are painted a creamy white for added emphasis. Because the room is narrow, it is painted a light color scheme to make it feel bigger than it actually is.

NEW YORK CITY TOWN HOUSE

Middle-class New Yorkers lived in brownstones and the poor were consigned to wretched tenements. At the top of the nineteenth-century economic heap were merchant princes, grande dames of high society, and outright robber barons. Unlike their fellow citizens, these rich and socially prominent lived in luxurious quarters—the New York City town house—designed by the preeminent architects of the day. Though essentially a rowhouse, the New York City town house transcended the genre by incorporating architectural splendor, large, airy rooms, and privacy.

The finest example of the New York City town house style is undoubtedly Colonnade Row, right, once the home and social headquarters of families such as the Vanderbilts and Astors. Colonnade Row has been stripped of much of its original architectural glory but it still bears eloquent witness to the days of laissez-faire when the wealthy did not have to pay federal income tax, or minimum wage to their employees. Colonnade Row was initially known as La Grange Terrace when it was built in 1836 as speculative housing for the rich. Designed by architect Alexander Jackson Davis, the structure occupied the length of an entire city block of what is known today as the Lower East Side. For the architectural envelope, Davis selected the opulence of marble and an equally impressive architecture—the Greek Revival style (see pages 134–37). Each of the nine residences was a self-contained unit with the entire row visually unified by columns spanning the length of the façade. When viewed from the street, the overall visual impression was that of a large mansion.

Besides linking the nine town houses, the towering, two-story columns added a sense of grandeur to the structure. The second and third floors were set behind the columns, which created a sweeping balcony. Like the more modest brownstone, the town house was designed with the public rooms on the second floor where they looked out onto the balcony. The importance of these rooms, as well as of the owner's bedrooms on the third floor, were emphasized by large-scaled, 6-over-6 windows. These brightened the interior and could be left open in summer for ventilation.

Like many later brownstones, town houses were entered at ground level through ornate doors flanked by columns. In most cases, arriving visitors entered a vestibule, then through a second set of double doors into the interior.

Today, Colonnade Row is drastically altered from its original form. Years ago, three of the nine town houses were demolished so that a department store warehouse could be constructed on the site. The six remaining town houses contain both commercial offices and residential lofts. Declared a landmark, the exterior of Colonnade Row is now protected from further alterations.

CAMP STYLE

The new fellowship hall of a Ukrainian church in Upstate New York embodies many of the architectural lines and materials of the Camp style including the long, low roof that becomes a porch overhang.

The gable-roofed dormer windows of this new house in the Catskill Mountains of New York State echo those of the Camp style.

In the late nineteenth century, the Gilded Age generated vast fortunes for the giants of manufacturing, many of whom were headquartered in New York City. Seeking an escape from the oppressively hot and humid New York summers, a number of these families took advantage of the advent of rail travel to the Adirondack and Catskill mountains and built out-of-town retreats in these unspoiled wilderness areas.

The simple log cabin (see pages 132–33) inspired the architectural styling for these summer residences. Instead of a plain, one-room structure, the architects of the wealthy designed vast estates—some can sleep more than 100 persons—so that entire families and their household staffs could move north for the summer and live in self-contained luxury.

The Camp style of architecture and furnishings is thoroughly documented in two excellent books, *Great Camps of the Adirondacks* by Harvey H. Kaiser and *American Rustic Furnishings* by Susan Osborn. Because of the enormous scale of the estates, which only great wealth could support, these houses and their furniture are dramatically different from virtually any other movement in American architecture and design. Perhaps the most honest reaction was Sigmund Freud's, who, as quoted by Ms. Osborn, bluntly said, "Of everything I have experienced in America, this is probably the strangest."

Some people might share that point of view. However, the construction and materials of many of the lodges are remarkable and indisputably eye-catching. In the nineteenth century, the style became so popular that it eventually spread from the mountains of Upstate New York to the buildings of Central Park in New York

Sagamore Lodge is the epitome of the Camp-style architecture that was popular in Upstate New York in the late nineteenth century.

Rustic furnishings fill Topridge, the Adirondack retreat of heiress Marjorie Merriweather Post.

City and to the Pacific Northwest. But the style is still associated with the mountains of New York State where the grandest of these structures were built.

Undoubtedly, one of the grandest examples of Camp-style architecture is Sagamore Lodge. It was designed by its first owner, William West Durant, who was a major architect of lodges in the Adirondacks. Built in 1893 of native wood and stone by local workmen, Sagamore Lodge typifies the Camp style by blending log construction with the roof shape and balconies associated with the architecture of Switzerland. It consists of a series of log buildings—main house, service buildings, greenhouse, and even a school—all connected by walkways.

Twenty-two servants maintained the lodge that boasted amenities many poor city dwellers went without all year long—toilets, hot water, and gas lighting. Furnishings fashioned from peeled logs and twigs were juxtaposed with Japanese lanterns and decorative accessories such as animal skins, guns, snowshoes, and fishing rods. The effect is eclectic, to say the least.

After decades of neglect and decay, many of the lodges in the Adirondacks are being rehabilitated. Fortunately, Sagamore Lodge has been preserved and serves as a highly popular conference center. It is listed on the National Historic Register.

Financially, it would be almost impossible to duplicate the great camps today. Yet they have served as an inspiration for the design of some modern houses that carry on the tradition. A house by Ric Weinshenck, which is more reminiscent of the architecture of the Catskills than that of the Adirondacks, is designed with a swooping gable roof much like the one at Sagamore Lodge. This roof, however, is enlivened by dormer windows. The walls are constructed of dark-stained wood that wrap around the structure to meet at a large, fieldstone fireplace chimney. Instead of balconies, multilevel decks grace the exterior.

The Camp-style influence is far more subtle indoors where the fieldstone fireplace and wood plank floors recall the nineteenth-century style. Wainscoting, another nineteenth-century detail, rings the living room. But instead of twig furniture, the owners of this house have chosen another sort of furniture associated with a casual, outdoor-oriented lifestyle—wicker.

DUTCH FARMHOUSE

Van Cortlandt Manor, a classic example of the Dutch farmhouse, was supplemented with a double staircase and large verandas reminiscent of Caribbean architecture.

Like their English counterparts, early Dutch immigrants brought along their historic architecture to the New World. Settling in the Hudson River valley of New York State as well as in Pennsylvania and New Jersey, they built quaint farmhouses that reflect a folk heritage rather than the grand architecture of mainstream European styles. Distinguished by steep gable roofs, rock walls covered with clapboard siding, and sometimes built with dormer windows, these houses often provided shelter for both farm families and their animals. Thus, they served as both house and barn.

The Dutch farmhouse was elegantly reinterpreted in rural New Jersey by architect Robert S. Bennett of Pennington, New Jersey. Like its stylistic ancestor, this new house has a steep gable roof, shiplap siding, and double-hung windows. Instead of rock, however, the walls of the main portion of the house are covered with a synthetic stucco that is extremely durable. While the architectural envelope and detailing reflect the charm of the old, the house is built to be comfortable and as maintenance-free as possible. The architect expanded on the traditional form by enlarging it with the addition of a wing. Set at a 90-degree angle to the main portion of the house, it contains a popular contemporary amenity—a master suite. The double-hung windows on this wing are over-scaled making this large house seem smaller and, thus, blend with the site.

However, it is on the rear elevation that the contemporary elements can be seen most vividly. Large windows brighten the interior while an expansive deck off the kitchen encourages the owners to dine outdoors. Dormer windows at the front and back illuminate the second-floor bedrooms.

Indoors, all similarity to the past ends. On the ground floor, the living-dining area is one sweep of space. To define the two areas within the same room, Bennett designed a loft for an at-home office above the living area.

A grander version of the Dutch farmhouse is the manor house, of which the best known example is Van Cortlandt Manor in Croton-on-Hudson, New York. Built as a small hunting lodge, Van Cortlandt Manor was enlarged over the years until it became the family seat in 1749. The house was occupied by the Van Cortlandt descendants for 200 years. Renovated and maintained by Sleepy Hollow Restorations, the Manor is open to the public.

The first floor, which was built in the 1600s, is the original portion of the house. It reflects the solid stone construction of the Dutch farmhouse and incorporates similar double-hung windows. The upper floors, with their typically Dutch steep-pitched roof, were added in the eighteenth century. The veranda, which is reached by a striking split staircase, was built in the 1800s.

The interior of Robert Bennett's interpretation of the Dutch farmhouse includes a study loft over the living area.

The façade of Bennett's new Dutch farmhouse is enlivened with a wing containing a large master suite.

FLEMISH HOUSE

The lines of the Dyckman House and other Flemish structures were freely interpreted in this century and sold by tract developers as "Dutch Colonial."

During the seventeenth century, a great migratory wave swept to America from Flanders, a small strip of territory now split between France, Belgium, and The Netherlands. Primarily farmers, the early Flemish immigrants settled on Long Island and in New Jersey where they built distinctive houses with large gable roofs and flared eaves extending out two or three feet.

Flemish settlers in the eighteenth century built gambrel-roof houses in New Jersey and in parts of New York. Unlike the English-inspired gambrel form, the Flemish variety was shorter at the top and less steeply pitched. New Jersey Flemish houses usually were built of stone while those in New York typically were a combination of stone and clapboard siding. The Dyckman House in New York City is an outstanding example of eighteenth-century Flemish architecture in the New World. It has a graceful gambrel roof, identical chimneys at each end, and fieldstone walls that rise to meet clapboard siding beneath the roof. On the façade, the roof overhang shields the front porch.

To most Americans, the appearance of the Flemish house will seem familiar. However, its "Flemish" designation will not. The reason is simple. The Flemish house was revived as "Dutch Colonial" architecture in the first half of the twentieth century. As Dutch Colonial, the style was favored by tract-housing developers. As a result, streamlined versions of this historic form abound in modern-day suburban America.

GERMAN STONE HOUSE

The German stonework tradition is rustically interpreted in the Hans Herr House in Pennsylvania.

The English were not the only people to bring Medieval building technology to the New World. The Germans who gravitated to Pennsylvania also erected houses with steep gable roofs, thick stone walls, and small windows. Whenever possible, the Germans built their houses over a stream or spring, thus supplying indoor running cold water and a refrigeration system for food.

The Hans Herr House in Lancaster County, Pennsylvania, incorporates all of these characteristics. Christian Herr built the house in 1719 as a home for his family as well as for Sunday worship for the local Mennonite settlement. It is named for Herr's father, Hans, who was the local Mennonite bishop.

This historic house measures 38 by 31 feet, and has massive exterior walls that are two feet thick. The roof is steeply pitched to accommodate a second floor and an attic. Heat was supplied by three different sources: on the first floor is a massive fireplace that measures 10 by 5 by 4 feet. It includes a masonry stone fireplace that heated the adjacent parlor. A smaller fireplace was used to warm the second floor.

The cellar was constructed as a vaulted arch of masonry that would have protected family members from injury if the house burned. The windows in the cellar are unusual. Measuring some thirty inches wide indoors, they narrow until they are no more than six inches wide on the outside.

One theory that explains the window construction asserts that they were intended as firing slits in case of Indian attacks. However, because the Herr family never installed a lock on the front door, that theory lacks credibility. In fact, the house was so open to outsiders and so snugly built that the Herr family often awoke on exceptionally cold mornings to find local Indians sleeping around the first-floor fireplace.

In 1969, the property was acquired by the Lancaster Mennonite Conference Historical Society, which began an ambitious restoration program. Today, the work is complete. Furnished to reflect life in colonial Pennsylvania between 1719 and 1750, the house is operated by the Mennonite Society as a museum and is open to the public.

CHAPTER

FOUR ■

Many persons' image of the architecture in the South may well be limited to visions of Tara from *Gone With the Wind*. Granted, many of the great antebellum mansions that the home of Scarlett O'Hara symbolized remain intact as private homes or museums. But there is much more to the architecture of this part of the country than the southern mansion. Humbler residences include the Dogtrot and the Shotgun houses. In a region overrun with tract houses placed haphazardly across the land, the ideas for cooling and ventilation embodied in the historic architectural examples of the South are as practical today as they were a century ago.

This plantation house, Shadows-on-the-Teche, is a fine example of the Southern mansion and of the Greek Revival architectural style.

PLANTATION HOUSE

Protected by a roof overhang, a deep veranda sprawls across one entire elevation of Mount Vernon. An outstanding example of the Southern plantation house, Mount Vernon is enhanced by Palladian windows.

The formal West Parlor of Mount Vernon suggests the splendor of the Southern colonial mansion.

Though we think of the typical Southern plantation house as a mansion, many were originally small houses that were enlarged as the families grew and their fortunes prospered. The owner's house served as the nerve center of a small empire surrounded by out-buildings such as the kitchen, smoke house, various workshops, stables, and slave quarters. Most of these estates were as self-supporting as possible eliminating the need to import or buy clothing, farm implements, and livestock. The work force consisted of slaves, most of whom tended the fields. Male slaves worked as blacksmiths, gardeners, carpenters, and painters. Slave women were servants, cooks, and seamstresses.

Plantation houses were built in a variety of architectural styles. An early example, the Adam Thoroughgood House in Virginia, was built around 1680 in the English Tudor style, as seen in the low, overhanging roof form and the unusual chimney design that is reminiscent of a pyramid. Most early plantation houses were built of wood. The Thoroughgood House, however, was built of brick. Now fully restored, it is maintained by The Chrysler Museum and is open to the public.

The most famous plantation house in America is Mount Vernon, the home of George and Martha Washington. Constructed as a small one-and-a-half story house with a central hallway and four small rooms on the first floor, the house was enlarged to assume its present configuration of two-and-a-half stories.

An amalgamation of architectural ideas, Mount Vernon incorporates classically inspired columns, Palladian windows, and a typically Southern-style veranda that sweeps across the façade of the house. The classical motifs were commonly pictured in eighteenth-century English architecture books to which Washington had access. Fine detailing is part and parcel of the construction. The most noticeable of these is the wood siding, which has beveled edges to evoke the sense of fine stonework.

The exterior of the San Francisco Plantation in Louisiana clearly shows the influences of the Victorian Age.

Most Southern plantations are antebellum; some, however, were built later. These later houses reflect the prevailing architectural style of the time they were constructed. For example, the visually striking San Francisco Plantation in Reserve, Louisiana, was built in the late nineteenth century and is imbued with the architectural flavor of the Victorian Age. Large verandas wrapping around the sides of the house are shaded by the roof extension, which, in turn, is supported by a row of columns. At the top of the structure are twin chimneys and paired dormer windows.

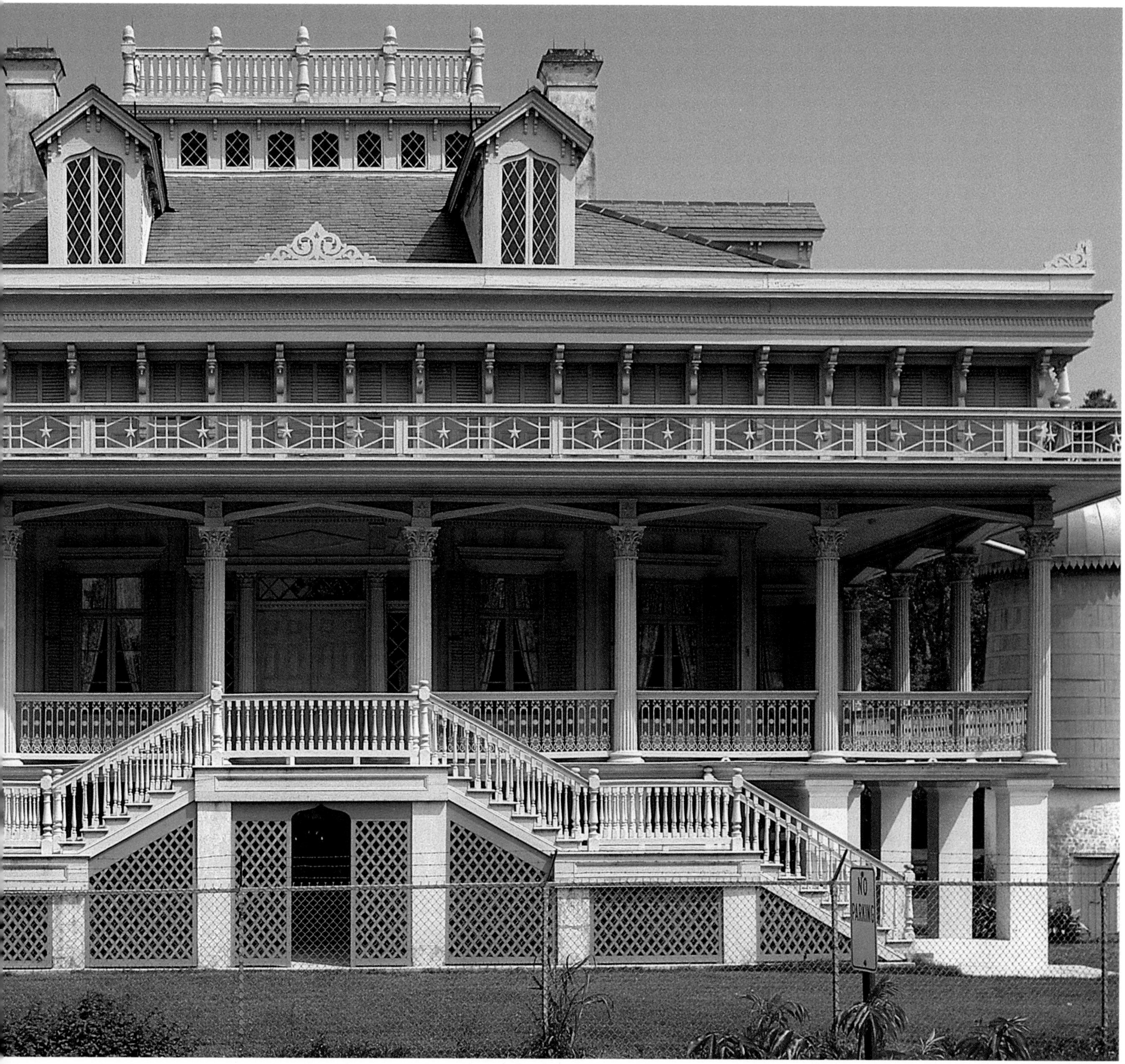
NO PARKING

CHARLESTON SINGLE

Indoors, the rooms are very traditional in their layout, with the living room at the front.

With its side facing the street, the Charleston Single makes the most of a narrow lot.

In the early nineteenth century, Charleston, South Carolina, was a booming commercial center. Because street frontage was at a premium, lots in Charleston, as in New York City, tended to be narrow and deep. As a result, many houses were extremely narrow. In fact, a number of them were one-room wide, giving rise to the designation Charleston Single.

For maximum outdoor living space, the Single was sited far to one side of the lot. Unlike most houses today, in which a wide façade faces the street, the two long sides of the Charleston Single ran from front to back. On one side, the house was augmented by a long veranda, or piazza, often topped by balconies. The veranda and balconies sheltered doors to the rooms. Thus, the doors could be left open in the heat of the day and even in rain storms. Windows located on the opposite long wall promoted cross-ventilation. For privacy, the veranda was shielded from street view by a door and entry that were often elaborately ornamented.

Thompson E. Penney's modern version of the Charleston Single is a clever abstraction of the prototype.

Though the Single was sited sideways, the interior layout is reassuringly familiar. On the ground floor, the formal entry was in the center of the house, flanked by the dining room at the back and the living room at the front. The formal room arrangement echoed the architecture. Much of the grace of the Charleston Single derives from its classical symmetry in the temple-like gable roof, paired window composition, and colonnaded piazza.

The Charleston Single has been imaginatively reinterpreted by architect Thompson E. Penney. Like its historic predecessor, the house Penney designed is one-room wide, oriented front-to-rear, and pushed to one side of lot. The architectural styling represents an abstraction of the original. The paired windows and long veranda are intact; geometric cut-outs in the exterior wall of the veranda and second-story balcony are reminiscent of the structural support columns gracing the prototype. At the same time, the openings are over-scaled to let more light in.

DOGTROT

The Dogtrot house is split through the center by a breezeway to which the rooms open, promoting flow-through ventilation.

One of the more ingenious methods of cooling in the days before air conditioning, the Dogtrot house originated in the southern Appalachian Mountain region. It is distinguished by an open breezeway that extends through the center of the house, off of which open the rooms. With this design, cooling breezes flow through the open core and into the rooms where windows on the exterior walls create' cross-ventilation.

Though few Dogtrot houses were built after the advent of central air conditioning, the energy crisis of the 1970s sparked a re-evaluation of the style. This vernacular architectural form has been updated and restated for today by Rowe Holmes Associates for a house in the semi-tropical climate of Tampa, Florida. In this modern version, the house is elevated eight feet above the ground to take better advantage of the breeze and to protect the house from flooding from a nearby tidal estuary.

Atop the house is a staple of Southern architecture—a belvedere—that is opened in warm weather to aid ventilation. Fans

The new Dogtrot retains the breezeway as a glassed-in living area.

The new Dogtrot house designed by Rowe Holmes Associates uses a belvedere and a metal roof for cooling in Tampa's hot climate.

draw hot air from the bedrooms through vents into the belvedere to assist this natural cooling system. The exterior walls of the house are wood, a traditional Florida building material until the introduction of concrete block. Another historically derived material is the tin roof, which became popular in the area around the turn of the century. The roof deflects the heat of the sun and its large overhang shades the exterior walls and windows.

The interior layout has been somewhat altered to accommodate modern-day life. For example, the traditional open breezeway has been designed as an enclosed living-dining-kitchen area. The ceiling rises to the roof peak promoting the movement of hot air up to the belvedere. Clerestory windows and a ceiling fan also encourage air circulation. The towering space draws the eye upward to make the space seem much larger than it actually is. This open-plan core is flanked by two enclosed rooms on each side that serve as areas for sleeping

A Texas hunting lodge by Frank Welch exploits the Dogtrot cooling strategy.

and hobbies. Additional bedrooms are on the second floor.

The Dogtrot idea has been adapted to meet a variety of shelter needs. A rustic, yet sophisticated Texas hunting lodge that was designed by architect Frank Welch is rendered in stone, which is a traditional—and plentiful—building material in the southern portion of that state. Otherwise, the structure has the architectonic look of a contemporary structure down to the multifunctional open area, which serves as a living and dining area near the massive fireplace. A deck provides a shady space to relax out of the harsh afternoon sun. Set on a hillside, the lodge both rises above its site and blends with it in the best traditional fashion.

The Dogtrot form is so versatile and practical that it can be built in a variety of materials—and with a great deal of creativity and wit. Texans take hospitality very seriously. So when architect Chris Carson of San Antonio was asked to design an entertaining space, he created a small work of art that is practical, regionally authentic, and a lot of fun.

The basic shell of the structure is reminiscent of a barn and, indeed, when the doors are closed, it looks much like a utilitarian farm structure. But come barbecuing time, doors are opened at each end to reveal a Dogtrot-inspired center breezeway that cuts a swath through the center of the structure. Indoors, the industrial ambience of the exterior gives way to ceramic tile floors, finely crafted woodwork, and modern, sliding glass doors. The juxtaposition and playfulness of the elements—commercial exterior, elegant interior, and a layout firmly grounded in age-old architectural principles—adds up to a flexible and thoroughly delightful structure that is in keeping with the best of modern design.

The Dogtrot configuration has been whimsically recreated by architect Chris Carson for a Texas-sized retreat—a party barn. The exterior is sheathed with commercial-type metal. The center Dogtrot opening is closed off by sliding glass doors, left. The opening serves as a dining area, right.

CAJUN COTTAGE

A distinct architectural house-type, the Cajun Cottage dates back to the French colonization of the Mississippi River valley. Named after the French Arcadian settlers who migrated down the Mississippi from Canada to the Louisiana Gulf Coast, the Cajun Cottage was tiny and primitive. Yet it embodied a touch of elegance in the form of a gallery that spanned the façade. The gallery was protected from sun by the overhang of the steeply pitched roof. Generally, the ground floor consisted of a single room, although more elaborate versions were extended to the rear with additional rooms. Above the ground floor was a loft that was reached by an open-tread exterior stairway placed at one end of the cottage. Also at that end of the house was the fireplace. Often these small dwellings had another amenity familiar to contemporary Americans—double, or French, doors composed of large shutters. For additional cooling, the small cottage was elevated, allowing the breeze to flow beneath the structure.

The influences of the Cajun Cottage can readily be seen in a new house by John Desmond. The steep roofline of this house echoes that of the Cajun Cottage as does the modern version of the gallery—a front porch shaded by the roof overhang. With the overhang providing shade, the windows could be enlarged to bring the view indoors. The exterior walls are painted white to reflect heat and the grounds are landscaped to provide shade.

A shady gallery enlivens the primitive lines of the Cajun Cottage.

The gallery in this new house is a common front porch.

FRENCH COLONIAL

A hip roof with flaring eaves marks French Colonial architecture.

The gallery was a favorite French motif. It is at its most developed in the French Colonial style where it sometimes wrapped around all four walls of the house. Other notable characteristics of this type of architecture are a hip roof surrounded by a lower-pitched roof over the gallery.

Perhaps the best example of this style—and the only one to be restored to its original state—is the Bolduc House in Ste. Genevieve, Missouri. Constructed around 1770 and moved to its present site in 1784, the house is a large rectangular building measuring 48 by 82 feet. Set on a stone foundation, the exterior walls are made of heavy timbers set vertically. The timbers were

placed six inches apart and the openings were filled with a mixture of clay and straw. The roof is supported by a system of heavy oak trusses reminiscent of French Medieval construction.

The interior of the Bolduc House consists of two large rooms separated by a central hallway. Originally, these were surrounded by the gallery, part of which was later enclosed to form the kitchen. The interior is decorated with examples of French-Canadian furnishings, including a few surviving pieces from the Bolduc family collection. The Bolduc House is operated by the National Society of Colonial Dames of America in the State of Missouri, and is open to the public during the summer.

SHOTGUN

These original Shotgun houses run straight from front to back without a hallway.

In many urban areas of the South, the cost of land and the need to conserve it led to the construction of houses only one room wide. One of these types is called the Shotgun because as the story goes, you could shoot a bullet from the front to the back of the house without striking a single wall.

The Shotgun house is a more modest relation of the New York City brownstone and the Charleston Single. Like the brownstone, the entry to the Shotgun house is on one side of the façade with adjacent windows overlooking the street. Though the Shotgun is a freestanding structure, it has no windows on the side walls. These houses are sited so close together that windows would

be impractical for light or ventilation and would severely compromise personal privacy.

The simplicity of the architecture belies its often evocative detailing. Many Shotgun houses have elaborately carved front doors and ornate entries imbued with classical motifs. Dentils beneath the eaves are decorated with lovely moldings and other wood-working details. The windows are often generously over-scaled to maximize the amount of daylight entering the rooms.

The interior is arranged in a simple fashion. Overlooking the street at the front of the house is the living room. Behind that is the kitchen with the bedroom and a small bath at the rear. There

A Victorian Queen Anne house echoes the form of the much more humble Shotgun.

are no interior hallways; instead, each room opens onto the next to maximize living space and, undoubtedly, to keep construction costs low. In larger versions, the Shotgun was built with a second floor at the rear to provide additional sleeping space.

In many Southern cities, the surviving collections of Shotgun houses face a grim future. Allowed to decay into a severe state of disrepair, today they are inhabited in many cases by only the poorest families. Yet because they are usually near a city's commercial core, the land they occupy has become highly valued. As a result, many of the remaining examples of this vernacular Southern architecture are probably doomed to be destroyed in coming years to make way for additional development.

There is one area in the South, however, where the modest Shotgun house has achieved nothing short of cult status—Louisville, Kentucky. There, the rich and diverse selection of these unusual structures has been preserved and recycled for new life today. Much of the credit for saving these distinctive houses belongs to the Preservation Alliance of Louisville and Jefferson County, Inc., the local historical society. Indeed, one entire block of Shotgun structures remains intact as residences, the 900 block of East Jefferson Street. Another area of the city rich in Shotgun houses is called Butchertown.

SOUTHERN RURAL

In a new community called Seaside, a development called Rosewalk by the team of Robert Orr and Melanie Taylor incorporates many of the traditional elements of Southern rural architecture.

Beginning in the late nineteenth century and lasting well into the twentieth century, the economic and social life of the South was centered not in the few, large cities, but in small rural towns. To cope with the hot, sultry weather, the wood-frame houses had expansive porches, tin roofs with deep overhangs, and large windows to ventilate the interior. These houses were tailor-made for the slower pace of life that was dictated by the weather and the agrarian-oriented lifestyle.

This approach to architecture has been reinterpreted in the 1980s. The site is the Florida Panhandle near Panama City, where the atmosphere is more rural Alabama than Miami Beach. Here, in the area known as the "Redneck Riviera," Robert Davis has developed a waterfront community called Seaside. Envisioned as a resort community, Seaside was planned by architects Andres Duany and Elizabeth Plater-Zyberk of Miami and brings together many of the homegrown, small-town qualities of the region— pedestrian paths and specific zones for houses, businesses, and public buildings.

Recently, an enclave of fourteen houses designed by architects Robert Orr and Melanie Taylor was built in Seaside. This development-within-a-development is called Rosewalk and occupies three acres overlooking the beach. The cottages and houses Orr and Taylor designed are typical of the bygone Southern rural vernacular tradition with their large front porches that direct the view toward the Gulf of Mexico. The structures fall into three categories: one-story cottages with a dormer, one-story cottages with a tower, and two-story houses. All of these houses are unified by compatible trim including latticework, brackets, and other Victorian-inspired details as well as a contemporary color scheme consisting of various shades of pale rose and yellow. Throughout Rosewalk, gazebos and other nineteenth-century—style structures encourage residents of the resort to mingle while taking in the view and lingering in the best Southern tradition.

Picket fences and long walkways recall the more leisurely pace of life associated with the Victorian Age.

MIAMI MEDITERRANEAN

Many elements of Miami Mediterranean style originate in South Europe. The white stucco motif works well in hot humid environments by reflecting the brilliant sun. The overhangs created by the extended roof provide shading for comfortable outdoor living.

Generous applications of floor tile and exposed ceiling beams recall Florida's Spanish heritage.

The tropical climate of South Florida is remarkably similar to that of Spain, Italy, and other Mediterranean countries. . When the great Florida resorts and winter houses of the rich Northerners were built in the early twentieth century, architects turned to the architectural tradition of these countries, particularly the classical and Renaissance periods. One of the grandest examples of this movement is Villa Vizcaya in Miami. Built in 1916, Vizcaya was the winter home of International Harvester vice-president James Deering. The scale of the house is vast as it consists of seventy rooms and four towers. Architect Paul Chalfin designed Vizcaya in the Italian Renaissance style with huge Palladian windows in pale stained glass, classical-style columns, and seventeenth-century—style marble floors. Vizcaya has been fully restored and is now open to the public as Vizcaya Museum and Gardens.

Vizcaya is an extreme example of this Mediterranean style of architecture in the American South. More common in South Florida are buildings heavily influenced by the region's Spanish dominated past. One of the most famous original houses of this type is the Ribera House in St. Augustine, Florida. The white plaster walls and the ornate, dark-stained woodwork on the balcony and

the shutters are typically Spanish. These blocked direct sunlight from the interior and shielded it from street view. To the side, an exterior doorway opens into a courtyard where a first-floor veranda wraps around the side and rear walls. Shaded by the second floor, the veranda served as an outdoor living space in warm weather. The Ribera House is part of a restored area of St. Augustine called San Agustin Antiguo. Operated by the Historic St. Augustine Preservation Board, the area contains several interesting houses that are open for public tours.

The influences of Florida's Spanish Colonial past are also seen in many newer houses. Houses in Coral Cables are topped with roofs of red Spanish tile much like those found in California with walls that are protected by an application of stucco. Indoors, the airy rooms are brightened by Palladian-inspired curved windows that lend the spaces a sense of formality. Offsetting this grandeur, and recalling the area's history as a fun-oriented resort, houses are often furnished with casual wicker and cushions in bright colors. Floors are covered with square tiles alternating in black and white, a popular motif of the 1920s. Ceiling beams in natural wood tones visually soften the sleek white walls.

CHAPTER
FIVE ■

The Southwest is a true melting pot of American architecture and furnishings. The influences on the houses of this region are many—from the Native Americans, who contributed many of the basic forms of the early adobe houses to architectural motifs from the Spanish settlers, and, finally, to the stylistic refinements imported from the East by American settlers.

In many parts of the Southwest, traditional architecture and design are alive and flourishing. In other areas, they have inspired the design of modern houses that deftly blend the best of the old with the best of the new.

A huge latticework screen shades the roof of this desert house to keep the interior cool even on the very hottest days. It is supported by massive timbers.

ADOBE

Penetrating the walls of many adobe houses in the Southwest are timbers called *vigas* that not only offer structural support but create arresting details.

Adobe is a particularly durable material made by blending soil, water, and straw. This mixture is placed in a wooden frame and left to dry in the sun into bricks. Though associated in America with the houses of New Mexico, Beverly Spears points out in *American Adobes* that the material also is used widely throughout the Mediterranean region and probably dates back to Mesopotamia. Indeed, even the word "adobe" is Arabic in origin.

Because the new settlers adopted this practical material for their own houses, adobe houses encompass a number of styles. One of the oldest is Spanish Colonial. Usually these houses were built with massive walls measuring two or three feet thick. The exterior was coated with a protective layer of whitewash while those on the interior were plastered with mud. Peeled logs were used for the ceiling; these were covered with branches and dirt. The floors were dirt, often covered with animal skins. Fireplaces were set in a corner of the room.

Typically, the Spanish Colonial adobe house was one-story high, one-room deep, and arranged around a square courtyard. Most rooms opened directly into the courtyard or patio. This arrangement preserved privacy from the street; in fact, outer walls were generally windowless to fortify the house against attack.

In the early nineteenth century, the Spanish Pueblo style became popular. Probably the best known Spanish Pueblo structure is the Palace of the Governors in Santa Fe, which is an excellent restored example of this style that is open to tourists.

A modern adobe house near Santa Fe retains the historic ceiling treatment of *vigas* topped by small latticelike *lattilas.*

The striking combination of adobe walls from the West and a hip roof and Victorian columns from the East results in an unexpected sense of eclecticism in this nineteenth-century New Mexico house.

Contemporary adobe houses often mix a number of traditional adobe motifs and architectural elements such as a flat facade, smooth walls and linear design into a style generally called Santa Fe.

A new house near Placitas, New Mexico, designed by architect Steve Earnest illustrates the enduring quality of the Spanish Pueblo style with its thick, solid adobe walls and pine *canales,* or gutters, at each corner.

The Palace of the Governors in Santa Fe is an outstanding example of the Spanish Pueblo style.

Early Anglo settlers also adapted the prevailing style of the time to the adobe material. Some of the first adobe houses built by Americans had steep, gable roofs and dormer windows reflecting East Coast influences. By the 1840s, adobe houses were being built in the Greek Revival style, complete with arches and classically inspired columns. In the 1880s, Victorian styles surged into favor. These were often embellished with gingerbread, columns, decorative woodwork, and even picket fences.

The influences of so many cultural forces and the rapid growth of available materials resulted in the design of houses that embody a number of different traits. Many of these older houses have been remodeled and new ones built to take advantage of the benefits of adobe—its insulating ability and its inherent linking of house, culture, and a sense of place.

Because the adobe house has been influenced by so many disparate sources, the modern structures built in this genre are varied, indeed. Reminiscent of the Spanish Pueblo style is an expansive modern residential compound near Santa Fe that incorporates the flat façade, smooth walls and, to a lesser degree, the linear design associated with that style. These create the visual impression of a long, narrow house, an image that is reinforced by retainer walls extending out to enclose courtyards off the major rooms. The Spanish Pueblo style also took root in Arizona where it is called the New Mexico Style.

ROCKY MOUNTAIN

Aspen architect William Lipsey here harkens back to the Rocky Mountain tradition by incorporating board-and-batten siding and a metal roof.

Bedroom furnishings are an artful blend of regionally inspired textiles and accessories with an imported Italian lamp.

Throughout the house, the windows are carefully positioned to make the most of the spectacular mountain view—even from the bath.

In the nineteenth century, great mining camps in the Rocky Mountains of Colorado served as the nerve centers of vast mining operations geared toward one goal—bringing the region's abundance of precious metals, including silver, to the surface. Today, most of the mining camps have been long abandoned, but they still have a firm hold on the architecture of the region. A number of architects have incorporated the motifs of the mines into their work. However, few have been as successful as William Lipsey of Aspen, whose houses meld historical architecture and furnishings, regional materials, and highly energy-efficient design.

Lipsey's own house serves as a lesson in the vernacular architecture of the Rocky Mountains. The exterior is clad with board-and-batten, a traditional building material in the region. As befitting a house built in an Alpine climate, the metal roof is set at a steep slope so snow falls easily to the ground. Most glazing faces south to take advantage of solar gain.

The interior of the Lipsey house has that remarkable quality of combining diverse styles of furnishings within a well-thought-out space-planning scheme.

In a sleeping area, exposed wood beams and a ceiling enlivened by a stained glass skylight visually warm the white walls. Like the living area, bedroom furnishings are native Rocky Mountain accessories eclectically blended with internationally influenced items such as an imported Italian lamp.

Wherever possible, Lipsey has opened the house to the outdoors. Besides maximizing solar gain, this design strategy exposes the interior to the panoramic view of mountains and meadows, making the house seem larger and lessening the sense of being trapped indoors during the winter. No opportunity to bring the outdoors into the interior is missed, not even in the bathroom where an expansive window with a stained glass insert provides a bather's-eye view of a mountain.

DESERT STYLE

In the Southwest, the climate ranges from the clear Alpine cold of the Rocky Mountains to the hot deserts of Arizona. Each climatic zone requires architecture that ensures comfortable living. The desert in particular offers an exacting challenge. In many ways, the Arizona desert is a climatic contradiction. During the day, temperatures can soar well above 100 degrees under the glaring sun. Often, the nights are surprisingly chilly.

The climatic extremes of the desert call for architecture that is particularly adept at balancing concerns for climate while still providing for livability and style. Traditional design provides for these, and many architects are turning to this precedent for inspiration. In designing a house in Arizona, architect Judith Chafee took ample advantage of the region's rich architectural heritage. Floating above the structure is an enormous screen that diffuses the glaring light of the sun. Constructed of wood, the screen extends over most of the house including enclosed and outdoor areas. Essentially a "double roof," the screen represents a Southwest desert tradition that was nearly lost after cheap fossil fuel made mechanical air conditioning affordable.

The screen serves a variety of purposes. Besides reducing the cooling load on the house by shading the structural roof, it incorporates slots that draw breezes downward. It also reduces the natural light level and allows the structure to have larger windows. In addition, the screen helps blend the large 4300-square-foot house with the landscape.

Structural support for the roof is supplied by twenty large wood timbers that soar through the interior. Rather than camouflage these structural elements, architect Chafee left them exposed and incorporated them into the main living areas. There, they serve as a subtle reminder of the unseen sunscreen. Both exterior and interior walls are made of block masonry that creates a highly textured visual effect indoors and out. The floor is covered with locally produced ceramic tile.

Heavy timbers rise through a house designed by Judith Chafee to support an enormous wood screen that shades the roof from intense sun.

NATIVE AMERICAN INFLUENCES

Many examples of Native American architecture have disappeared. Those that remain are prized reminders of the region's cultural heritage and are the focus of preservation efforts. There are a number of reasons for the disappearance of Native American architecture. Much of it was transient in nature, especially the dwellings of the nomadic tribes. Others disappeared because of the nature of the building materials. The Pueblos, for example, used a form of earth construction before the Spanish colonization of New Mexico. However, it was pressed damp clay, which is less durable than adobe.

Yet the architectural influence of the Native Americans can be found in contemporary Southwest houses. Architect Morton Hoppenfeld turned to this rich source of imagery when he designed a house in Albuquerque that is at once of-the-moment and a whimsical interpretation of the native Southwestern building tradition. While the walls of the house look as though they are constructed of mud, they are actually stucco that has been applied to create a lumpy appearance, then painted in earth tones. The spare landscape may strike the casual observer as excessively barren. Consisting of raked earth and water, it helps blend the building plot with the surrounding land so well that one is not quite certain where the yard ends.

The interior is a pleasing mix of contemporary architecture and regional materials. The multi-shed roof rises to create airy volumes in the living and dining areas in the best modern manner. The materials, however, echo another era with their brick floors and white plaster walls. The dining area is a lean-to sunspace that is protected from excessive light and heat levels by lattice-work screening on the exterior. The towering fireplace is arranged so that it can be viewed from both the dining area and the kitchen.

A traditional whitewashed wall soars to new and contemporary heights.

Architect Morton Hoppenfeld adapted the elements of Native American architecture—water and mud—into a modern house near Albuquerque.

The Midwest is an anomaly in American architecture. Though old (several states in this region of the country were admitted to the Union soon after the founding of the Republic), the Midwest has few indigenous architectural styles. For the most part, the hardy people who settled the Ohio Valley and the surrounding areas reproduced the architecture of the East.

There are, however, two completely different styles that sprang from this part of the country that have influenced architecture throughout America—the Ohio farmhouse and the Prairie Style that was popularized by Frank Lloyd Wright. The farmhouse strongly influenced the design of structures built throughout the region and as far south as Texas. The reputation of Wright, who has been called America's greatest architect, transcends a single region. In fact, it was the vision of Wright and his contemporaries that helped usher in the era of the modern American house.

With its low profile and extended space, the Prairie School house revolutionized the look of American residential architecture.

OHIO FARMHOUSE

The Ohio farmhouse
has been imaginatively
updated by Washing-
ton, D.C., architect
Hugh Newell Jacobsen.

The rural wood-framing and white paint are enlivened with stylized lightning rods and a centrally placed skylight.

The vernacular domestic architecture of rural Ohio can be summed up succinctly—wood-frame, white, and adorned with numerous gables in the tradition of the nineteenth century. This is the sort of house that comes to mind when Americans who grew up before World War II think of their grandparent's farm. In keeping with the Victorian tradition, the rooms were large. Fireplaces in each of the two parlors on the first floor warmed family members in winter and provided a center for socializing. A sweeping porch across the façade served as an outdoor living room where children and adults lazed away hot summer afternoons in the shade and visited after dinner.

The Ohio farmhouse has been rendered in a startlingly contemporary fashion by architect Hugh Newell Jacobsen of Washington, D.C. The house incorporates all the prerequisites of the Ohio farmhouse including a small "barn," which is actually the garage on the first floor and a guest suite on the second floor.

Rectangular in shape, the house is visually enlivened by gables and five bays with 10-foot-high windows. The exterior cladding is sparkling white board-and-batten while the roof is constructed of another traditional material—tin. On the roof are lightning rods that will be familiar to anyone who has traveled throughout the Midwest. A cupola made of glass crowns the roof to pour light into the core of the house.

In addition to the traditional gables, this contemporary house has four symmetrically placed fireplace chimneys and a large front porch. Furnished with beautiful white wicker chairs, tables, and the obligatory swing, the porch adds to the large amount of interior living space and shades the first-floor living room and dining room from the heat of the summer sun. A breezeway enclosed in glass connects the house and the garage.

This new "farmhouse" incorporates an old element—a front porch. Protected by an overhang, the porch is a relaxed setting for taking in the sun and informal entertaining.

The crisp white color scheme is carried through to the indoors where, again, Jacobsen has blended new and old in an exciting way. The floor-to-ceiling windows maximize the view and the simple, old-time window treatment of louvered shutters allows both sashes to be concealed for greater control over interior light levels. Contrasting with these traditional elements is a contemporary lighting scheme that eschews grandmother's proliferation of shaded lamps for ceiling fixtures.

The window bays are used in a number of ways. They are fitted with desks in the children's rooms while in the second-floor master suite, the bay neatly accommodates a whirlpool tub providing bathers with a panoramic—and private—outdoor view.

PRAIRIE SCHOOL

Unlike the Victorian house, which soared upward to a hot attic, the Prairie School house hugged the ground and extended outward—in this case, to the street—recalling the prairies of the American Midwest.

As the 75-year-long Victorian Age progressed, houses became more ornate. By the late nineteenth century, many were burdened with layers of gingerbread decoration or other unnecessary effects, which gave them an unpleasant, jumbled appearance.

About that time, a new approach to architecture emerged in the Midwest—the Prairie School—that was to end the days of the Victorian house and usher in the modern house as we know it today. Unlike the soaring Victorian house, the Prairie School house hugged the ground and extended out horizontally, recalling in many peoples' minds the prairies of the region.

Walls functioned as screens and were punctuated with bands of windows on the upper floors to take advantage of the view. Instead of opening up-and-down many windows swung out to embrace the landscape. The roof was redefined as an umbrella for the house. Set at a gentle slope, it extended outward with large overhangs. Often, the roof was pierced with skylights allowing shafts of light to filter indoors.

The living area was placed on an upper level where it commanded a view and was exposed to the breeze. A broad fireplace was often at the very center of the design. Boxlike rooms were rearranged into a free-flowing open plan. By minimizing the number of interior walls, architects enhanced the flow of light and air through the interior while lowering construction costs. This also made the house seem larger by allowing one area to visually "borrow" space from adjoining ones. To reinforce this effect, moldings and threshold saddles, which signal the end of one space and the beginning of another, were eliminated. Because they define space rigidly, right-angle corners were avoided in favor of other shapes—diagonals, diamonds, circles, and arcs.

The number of materials was also limited so that individual interior spaces were unified into large units. And, finally, to blend the house with its site and minimize the barrier between the indoors and the outdoors, the structure was stretched out into the landscape beyond the main envelope. Architects achieved this effect by continuing the materials specified for the house in low exterior walls, walks, and terraces.

What made these ideas possible was the technology developed during the Victorian Age. Precast concrete provided support for many houses, making interior structural walls unnecessary and promoting the adoption of open planning. The development of plate glass encouraged the design of large windows. Central heating compensated for warmth lost through the increased amount of glazing. The invention of electricity eliminated the need for larders and root cellars, thus streamlining and reducing the size of service areas such as the kitchen.

Though embraced by a number of architects, the Prairie School reached its zenith in the work of Frank Lloyd Wright. Wright designed his first house—for himself—in 1887. By the time he died in 1959, he had designed more than 1000 buildings, of which 650 were houses. Each of them embodies Wright's idea that a house should represent more than mere shelter. In fact, he believed that

Frank Lloyd Wright designed large light globes for the living room of the Robie House that simulate the illumination provided by sunlight.

a well-designed house could inspire the owners to vastly improve their personal lives. As he put it, "To make a dwelling place a work of art—this is the American opportunity."

Throughout his career, Wright's work remained uniquely American. While other architects copied European prototypes including English castles, French *chateaux,* and the pipe-railed houses of the Bauhaus architects, Wright's houses were low to the ground with broad eaves that reached down to the terrain

Strong horizontal lines distinguish Wright's Robie House.

of the true heartland of America, the Midwest.

One of the best examples of Wright's work is the Robie House in Chicago. Maintained by the Office of Special Events at The University of Chicago, the Robie House was designed in 1906 and build during 1908 and 1909 for a manufacturer, Frederick C. Robie, who was twenty-seven, when Wright was thirty-seven years old.

The Robie House incorporates the essence of the Prairie School with its strong horizontal lines and overhanging windows on the exterior, and interior spaces that are free-flowing. Because of the hovering roofs and projecting balconies, the house appears to be a series of planes floating in space. The only strong vertical element is the chimney, which was the first part of the house to be built followed by construction of the side walls.

The overhangs created by the balconies and the roof eaves shielded walkways from rain, snow, and summer sun on three sides of the house. The brick construction is visually softened by the inclusion of pockets for plants in the terrace walls.

The living room is on the second floor and separated from the adjacent dining room by the central fireplace. For the living room, Wright designed a lighting system that even today would

**A combination dining-
sitting area illustrates
the open floor plan.**

be unusual. Extending nine feet into the room along the north
wall was a screen supporting large light globes that provided
general illumination called "sunlight." For a more subdued effect,
the screen included grillwork, which consisted of long strips of
oak and crosspieces through which subdued illumination, called
"moonlight," simulated light filtering through tree branches.
Though this level of lighting was much lower than that supplied
by the globes, it was calibrated so that it was sufficient for most
activities. The design of the lighting system enabled the owners
to turn on the moonlight, sunlight, or both.

The interior is zoned with the living room, dining room, and
kitchen grouped together. On the second floor is a guest bedroom
and bath, which is separated from the master bedroom and children's rooms on the third floor to insure the Robie family privacy,
even when entertaining weekend guests.

Wright's work influences American architects today, some
quarter-century after his death. His ideas—open planning, easy
access to the outdoors, and the imaginative use of natural materials—are accepted by contemporary architects who almost always incorporate them into their own work.

CHAPTER

SEVEN ∎

The architecture of the West is startling in its variety. The Bay Area Style found in the San Francisco area is indisputably home-grown. The many Victorian houses in that city reflect a unique regional interpretation of the nineteenth-century styles that were popular across America. In Los Angeles and San Diego, the architecture is heavily laced with the flavor of Spain and Mexico. Juxtaposed with the sophisticated urban styles of building is the rougher texture of the sod houses of the old West that have been documented in Idaho and surrounding states.

Many house-types and styles of the West have been relegated to history. Examples of other styles are being remodeled creatively while new interpretations continue to be built. In some areas of the West—Los Angeles comes immediately to mind—avant-garde architects make the West one of the most interesting regions of the country.

Informal, set low to the ground and surrounded by verandas, the bungalow flourished all over the country but was most popular in California.

BAY AREA STYLE

The California redwood in the Buckeye House, an outstanding example of the Bay Area Style, is contrasted by a generous use of glazing.

Indoors, the Buckeye House is enhanced by dramatic sloping ceilings, exposed redwood ceiling beams and window trim, and thoroughly Californian wicker furnishings.

In San Francisco, individuality is not so much tolerated as it seems to be a civic responsibility. It comes as no surprise then that individuality flourishes in architecture. One of the indigenous styles of the counties surrounding San Francisco is appropriately labeled the Bay Area Style. Like the West in general, the Bay Area Style blends the formality of classically inspired details, such as classical columns, into informal living spaces made from local materials, and an overall simple, informal approach to design.

The Buckeye House is a case in point. Designed by architect Stephen Lubin, it appears to hug the ground and is centered around the swimming pool. Natural materials predominate with shingles made of California redwood comprising the roof and exterior walls. The landscaping emphasizes local plant varieties: oak trees, wisteria, roses, berries, and chestnut-like buckeye trees.

Strung along the wall facing the swimming pool is a two-story gallery. In the traditional manner it serves as a hallway linking the dining room and kitchen with the living room at the opposite end of the house. But the gallery is much more serviceable than its original prototype. Because it is set below grade, the gallery "draws" the second-floor bedrooms closer to the ground. It also serves as a heat sink that absorbs solar warmth for winter space heating. In summer, the owners open the windows in the gallery to efficiently cool the interior.

The one thoroughly modern aspect of this house is that it incorporates two solar heating systems. One is active, consisting of solar panels on the roof that heat the swimming pool; the other is passive, and is made up of forty tons of masonry carefully placed within the structure to absorb the warmth of the sun.

SAN FRANCISCO VICTORIANS

San Francisco's old Victorian houses offer highly detailed façades to public view.

A variety of Victorian architectural styles proliferated during the nineteenth century. But nowhere in America did they flourish as much as in San Francisco. The reasons are simple. Most of the city was built during the second half of the 1800s when the Victorian Age was at its height; and like many other urban areas in America, San Francisco was laid out in long, narrow lots by early city planners. This encouraged homeowners to build Victorian houses, which maximized living space by rising vertically rather than spreading horizontally.

The nineteenth-century houses of San Francisco embody many of the same mainstream Victorian styles found throughout the United States. However, there are some significant differences that distinguish San Francisco's "Painted Ladies" from similar Victorian houses in other regions. For example, to compensate for the steep hills in the city, houses included large bases creating a level building platform. Because of the configuration of the building plots, the only prominent place for architectural embellishment was on the street-facing façade. As a result, these houses tend to be more detailed on the front than similar styles in other parts of the country. Elaborate detailing, which is a hallmark of American interpretations of English Victorian styles, has been put to eye-catching advantage by the modern owners. In many cases, they have highlighted the carpentry by painting it in an array of bright or unusual combinations of colors.

Finally, the sheer number of Victorian houses in San Francisco add to their architectural distinction. Before the 1906 earthquake, there were an estimated 20,000 to 30,000 Victorian houses in San Francisco. Though fires generated from the earthquake destroyed 514 blocks of Victorian houses, some 14,000 of these remain standing today.

In San Francisco, three Victorian styles predominate: Italianate, Eastlake-Stick, and Queen Anne. These three styles can be classified by periods in San Francisco architecture. The Italiante Victorian house was popular between 1850 and 1875. It is most easily identified by its flat roof. Generally, the façade is either flat or enlivened with bay windows, a regional design motif. Unlike a porch or balcony, which is topped by a light-blocking overhang, the bay window captures sunlight and allows it to brighten the interior, a decided plus in San Francisco where the days are often enshrouded in fog. The bay window also brings the view indoors while shielding the interior from uncomfortably cool seabreezes.

The Italianate house also can be identified by the thin columns that resemble the straight lines of a smoking pipe. These pipe-stem columns, as they are called, often flank the front door. They are usually found in combination with cornices, panels, and brackets under the eaves.

The Italianate evolved into an architecture that blended the Stick and the Eastlake styles. The degree to which any single style dominates varies from house to house. Those reflecting Stick style architecture have bay windows that are squared and geometric. Doors and windows were visually highlighted by trim,

usually made of redwood. The Eastlake influences are extensive ornamentation and recessed decorative panels. To make the Victorian houses of San Francisco truly different from those in other parts of the country, some nineteenth-century architects also topped Stick- and Eastlake-style houses with French-inspired mansard roofs (a roof of four sides, each being of two slopes, the lower one steeper than the upper).

The Victorian Queen Anne house emerged as a popular San Francisco architectural style in the 1890s. The flat roof was replaced with the gable variety while the bay windows were reinterpreted as curves and set at the corners of the house. Detailing favors the naturalistic with wreaths and garlands rendered in plaster as the dominant motif.

The city's Italianate Victorian house has a flat roof and, often, bay windows, left. A gable roof and recessed decorative panels are the hallmarks of Eastlake influences, above.

CALIFORNIA BUNGALOW

Furniture and built-in cabinetry and serving surfaces in the famous Gamble House are all custom designed.

Indigenous to India, the first bungalows were simple, informal houses set low to the ground and surrounded by verandas. In the late nineteenth century, this type of house was transplanted to America where it flourished from 1900 to 1925. Though the bungalow was refined on the East Coast, it quickly spread across the country, reaching its zenith in California.

Bungalows were built in a number of architectural styles—from pseudo-Swiss to the Prairie School. Regardless of their architectural styling, all bungalows had certain characteristics in common. The structure itself was designed to be an informal, single-story house that was low to the ground. The floor plan greatly reduced the number of interior hallways, with rooms opening directly into each other. The low-pitched roof had deep eaves. Building materials included various indigenous woods, which primarily were left natural. In California, many bungalows were designed in a U-shape around a central courtyard.

Touted in the design and architecture press of the early twen-

tieth century, the bungalow possessed a number of advantages over other types of houses. For example, proponents cited that the single-story layout was space saving as it eliminated the need for a stairwell. Also, the simplicity of the overall design greatly reduced construction costs, which was one reason the bungalow proliferated across the country. Indeed, the bungalow was associated in most people's minds with reasonably priced housing for the middle class—"the ideal house at an affordable price."

The bungalow may have been thought of in terms of supplying simple, middle-class shelter but in the proper architectural hands, it was capable of achieving a great sense of style. Two brothers, architects Charles S. and Henry M. Greene built one of the finest examples of the bungalow in Pasadena, California, in 1903. In addition, it is an excellent example of the Arts and Crafts Movement in architecture and interior design (see pages 201–3). The Gamble House in Pasadena was the home of David B. Gamble of the Proctor and Gamble fortune. The exterior is a study in

Southern California building materials—redwood, cobblestone, masonry, board-and-batten siding, and leaded glass. Structurally, the Gamble House reflects influences of the Swiss and Japanese wood-building tradition. The low angle of the gable roof atop one wing is typically Swiss; at the other end of the house, an over-scaled overhang bespeaks the vernacular buildings of Japan.

These elements are deftly woven into an exuberant expression of the Southern California lifestyle. Wide terraces and open sleeping porches encourage indoor-outdoor living; deep eaves protect the interior from the hot sun; and careful siting takes maximum advantage of cross-ventilation and breezes. Elegant joinery, exposed structural timbers, and shingles create a sense of architectural detailing and help blend the house with the site.

The interior reflects the influence of the Arts and Crafts Movement in America. Begun in England by William Morris near the end of the nineteenth century, this approach to architecture and design sought to counteract the excessive and fussy decorating of the middle Victorian period when achieving high style meant filling houses with massive, ornate, machine-made furniture. The Arts and Crafts Movement stressed lightly scaled designs and handcraftmanship in the carving, joinery, and finishing of furniture.

This remodeled bungalow is brightened by new glazing under the gables.

In California, the bungalow court is an early twentieth-century tradition.

Residences such as the Gamble House made the reputation of Greene and Greene. Unfortunately, Greene and Greene houses succeeded too well. Their beauty attracted the attention of other architects who copied their designs resulting in the construction of misunderstood renditions of the brothers' work. As these houses were built, the Greenes lost commissions and the pair was largely forgotten by 1915. Designated as a National Historic Landmark, the Gamble House belongs to the City of Pasadena and the University of Southern California. It is open to the public.

The bungalow also lent itself to more humble interpretations. By the turn-of-the-century, many bungalows were grouped into courts in Southern California. Typically, a court was composed of several small, detached bungalows around a common walkway. In Pasadena one of these courts has been admirably preserved. It consists of five bungalows that were once rented out by the Hotel Maryland. Later, the bungalows were moved to another lot where for the next half-century they gradually decayed. A few years ago, the entire court was purchased by architect Philip Charles Lynch who undertook a complete rehabilitation program before reselling the structures to new owners.

Much of the work was devoted to improving the site. To create the effect of a forest glade, some thirty-five trees were planted. The flat plot was reshaped to form undulating earth berms that give the landscape a sense of character. The original straight-lined walkways were rerouted along these curves.

The interiors of the bungalows were updated by removing ceilings so that they rise to the roofline. Contemporary skylights were installed and glass was added in the gables overcoming one of the chief complaints about the structures—their dark interiors. Kitchens were fitted with skylights and were expanded to include service porches.

WESTERN FARMHOUSE

This contemporary house in Washington State embodies the shed roofs, large porches, and wood-framing of the Western farmhouse.

Skylights and a brick wall add interest to the kitchen, housed in the shed extension.

Large porches that wrap around three sides of the structure, low-pitched roofs sometimes topped with sod, and shed roofs characterize this style of architecture. The farm houses of Montana inspired a family to have a custom version built for themselves in Olympia, Washington. They contacted Robert Slenes of BJSS/Architects Planners, who retained the historic characteristics of this housing type while restating it in a thoroughly contemporary fashion.

The house is sited to take advantage of a view of Puget Sound. On the rear elevation, a frontier-style porch protected by a deep overhang flows around three sides of the living room. Set on two levels, the porch descends near the ground in front of the living room to leave sight lines clear. One step down from the porch is a traditional patio for sunning and informal entertaining.

Skylights set in the roof illuminate both the porch and the living room. A row of windows and glass doors allow additional light into the interior, creating an airy atmosphere. In the living area, the ceiling reaches upward. Clad with wood, it adds a sense of warmth to the contemporary house. That feeling is reinforced by a large brick fireplace and casual furnishings. A shed-roof extension contains skylights that brighten a large kitchen.

SOD HOUSE

Building materials were so scarce in some parts of the West that settlers resorted to building their primitive houses from soil.

In Montana and Idaho where timber was often in short supply, German and Russian immigrants adapted the building materials at hand to create their houses. Often, that required constructing houses of soil. Like their southwestern counterpart, the adobe house, sod structures offered insulation from cold in the winter and heat in the summer. The material was plentiful and could be fabricated into sturdy structures that would protect frontier families until they could afford to build more substantial housing.

Admittedly humble, these houses defy stylistic categorization. In their most primitive state, they were essentially dugouts. Resembling a large mound, the dugout could be distinguished from its surroundings only by a simple plank door and a small chimney. Sometimes, tiny windows were cut into the soil and framed in wood to enable light to penetrate the interior.

Sod houses were constructed of soil cut in bricklike form. Doorways were framed in first, then the bricks were arranged layer-upon-layer to create the walls. In some cases, the sod walls were framed in with lumber and covered with clapboard.

The energy crisis of the 1970s inspired a reevaluation of the idea of building with earth. The tradition of earth-sheltering was chosen by architect Gerald Yurk in designing his own house. In this case, the earth is used in the form of berms on three sides. Like the sod dugout, Yurk's house is built some four feet below grade to take advantage of the earth's natural tendency to retain summer heat into the winter and winter coolness far into the summer. Earth excavated for the construction was reshaped into the berms, which were built up another four feet for a total depth of eight feet. Though the Yurk family literally burrows in for the winter, their quarters are by no means primitive. Light enters the interior through windows set in the roof and via a two-story solarium containing a pool.

This "sod house" designed by Gerald Yurk has an indoor pool.

Today, building with soil, called "earth-sheltering," is one way to cut energy costs.

HISPANIC TRADITION

Architect Rob Quigley freely mixed the materials of California's Hispanic building past—adobe and tile—with geometric forms reminiscent of a Moorish style in designing this San Diego house.

Mexican tile visually softens the industrially inspired pipe railing used indoors.

The influence of Spain and Mexico on the architecture of California reaches back to the very roots of the settlement of the state. In the mid-eighteenth century, Spanish explorers constructed the familiar Pueblo-style missions that set the architectural tone for many public buildings. particularly during the early part of the twentieth century. The California ranch house of the nineteenth century is the clearest reminder of the Spanish Colonial tradition. Generally, it was constructed of adobe and topped with a low-pitched gable roof. Early ranch houses were a simple rectangular box; later, this central core was enlarged with a wing at each end.

This created a front patio area enclosed on three sides.

A fixture of post-World War II American suburbia, the modern ranch-style house is based on the ninteenth-century California prototype. Credit for creating the twentieth-century ranch house is generally given to Clifford May, who, not surprisingly, lives in one. May grew up in the San Diego area in an adobe house, the design of which inspired him when he built a house on speculation in 1931. It was the first ranch-style house and cost $9500.

"The ranch house was everything a California house should be," May told Joseph Giovannini of *The New York Times* in a 1986

Left open to the view, an adobe wall becomes a sculpture in a house remodeled by architect Ted Smith.

article. "It had cross-ventilation, the floor was level with the ground, and with its courtyard and the exterior corridor, it was about sunshine and informal outdoor living." Its emphasis on casual outdoor living meshed perfectly with the lifestyle of the 1950s, and May sold plans for some 18,000 ranch houses. His designs were also adapted by countless tract developers and contractors.

Today, the Spanish tradition remains potent in the architecture of Southern California. Many new houses embrace its geometric forms and materials, especially stucco. Rather than simply copy historic forms, the architects who design these houses are enlivening them with compatible, yet widely diverse, motifs.

Architect Rob Wellington Quigley blended Spanish and Moorish elements in designing a house in the Fairbanks Ranch development in San Diego. The Spanish Colonial influence is evident in the series of courtyards outdoors and in the double stairways indoors. The walls are stucco and the roof is tile. The geometric

Indoors, regional motifs give way to modern furnishings specified by interior designer Kathy McCormick.

archways echo the architecture of the Mediterranean.

The airy interior reflects the palette of the Southwest in its reddish-brown Mexican tile floors, rose-colored walls, and brown trim. In a bold departure from tradition, however, the stairways and interior balcony are outlined with industrially inspired pipe railing, giving the house a distinctly contemporary air.

An entirely different blend of Spanish and Moorish architecture can be seen in a remodeled residence near San Diego. Originally a small structure of wood and cinder blocks, the house today faces the street with a Mission-inspired wall. An arch in the wall leads into a courtyard and a new entry. The rambling floor plan of the interior recalls the ranch style. At the center of the house is the living room. The kitchen, family room, and bedrooms, including a separate master suite, are off the living room. One of the most striking parts of the residence is the pool house, which clearly reflects Moorish motifs with its latticework screening.

CHAPTER
EIGHT ■

Some architectural styles transcend a single region. The reason such styles become popular across the land varies from era to era. In the early years of the nineteenth century, for example, the Greek Revival style, which has been labeled America's first national architecture, was adapted from a classical form that possessed a sense of a past that the young United States lacked.

Today, many architects draw upon regional styles for inspiration. Others have taken a different tack. Some are embellishing basic International-Style buildings with motifs from the past and creating Postmodern architecture. Others are exploring how to incorporate age-old energy-generating and -saving techniques into structures that offer high style yet comfort.

These contemporary movements in architecture are exciting. Whether the style is as old as Greek Revival or as new as Postmodern, America's national styles influence the houses we build today, and thus, the way many of us live.

The enduring appeal of historic Greek Revival architecture is readily seen in this striking rooftop retreat.

LOG HOUSE

The log cabin may be the most venerated house-type in America. Indeed, presidential campaigns of the 1800s commonly stressed the candidate's birth in a log cabin as a not-so-subtle assurance to voters of his humble and thoroughly American origins.

What is not so American—at least in *its* origins—is the log cabin. It was brought to the Delaware River Valley during the 1660s by Swedish immigrants, and is a direct descendant of the

An old log house at the Finnish Farmstead at Old World Wisconsin has been expertly restored and is open to the public.

ancient Scandinavian log-building tradition. It was also a practical housing solution in the East as the basic building supplies—trees and rocks—had to be cleared from the land for farming.

America proved such fertile ground for the log house that the form moved west from the Eastern Seaboard along with the line of the advancing frontier. As a result, the log house may be the most ubiquitous house-type in America.

At its simplest, the log house was built in the American colonial tradition as a one-room cabin. Additional rooms were built on one side or as a second floor to enlarge the structure. Easy to build and admirably suited to primitive living conditions, the log house was used by many other ethnic settlers.

As the log house was appropriated by other groups around the country, it was adapted to a variety of climatic and cultural conditions. Logs were the material of choice for many humble dogtrot houses in the South as well as for many ranch buildings in the West. The rustic Adirondack style popularized in upstate New York also is an outgrowth of the log-house tradition.

Log houses continue to be built today. Entire magazines are devoted to the techniques of building and decorating these examples of rustic American architecture. Several manufacturers sell log houses in kit form that can be built by a contractor or by the purchaser himself. These newer versions are, in most cases, anything but primitive. Almost all are designed with open plans and many have two-story living areas. They can be equipped with an array of optional amenities such as whirlpool tubs, wet bars, state-of-the-art kitchens, skylights, and attached greenhouses.

Many new log houses are anything but cabinlike with open-plan interiors and two-story living areas that soar to cathedral ceilings.

Though this log cabin is imbued with the spirit of the old, it is a popular new kit house manufactured and sold by Timber Log Homes, Inc.

GREEK REVIVAL

Built in 1864, the Banning House in California utilizes regional redwood timbers for the frame.

When the locals visit Wyoming's Bank Club Bar, they enjoy a bit of Americana that stretches from one coast to another.

Before the dawn of the Victorian Age, architecture and the decorative arts were under the influence of eighteenth-century classicism. It was into this era of classicism that the United States emerged as an independent country. Classicism fit the perceived need to give a rough, young nation a sense of age-old grandeur.

The era of the Greek Revival lasted from approximately 1820 to 1850. Throughout America, examples of Greek Revival architecture can be found from structures as diverse as grand residences to local bars. Two of the greatest examples of Greek Revival residences are Andalusia, which was the Bucks County, Pennsylvania, home of Nicholas Biddle, and the Joseph Bowers

House in Northampton, Massachusetts. The architecture and interior design of these houses were of a piece—the classical detailing was continued indoors where furnishings were lightly scaled, creating an appearance of delicacy and grace.

The Greek Revival house reflects the temple-like form associated with classical buildings. The design of the roof and the columns are the most identifiable characteristics of Greek Revival architecture. Generally, it is a two- or three-story house with a low-pitched gable roof. Windows are recessed behind porches, which wrap around the front and sides. Sheltered by the overhanging roof, the porches are supported by rows of columns in

William Rawn offset the classical Greek Revival style with an asymmetric porch in designing this new house in Massachusetts. Instead of columns, it has decorative pilasters on the exterior walls.

groups of six or eight on each side. Like all classical columns, those incorporated into Greek Revival architecture consist of a base, shaft, and capital. Above that is the entablature, which consists of an architrave, frieze, and at the very top, the cornice. The frieze is usually ornamented with classically inspired sculpture.

Though classical motifs are often thought of as immutable and unchanging, Greek Revival architecture was interpreted in a variety of ways. Andalusia, for example, was a fairly straightforward copy of actual Greek temple architecture. As the style spread West with the country's boundaries, it took on distinct regional overtones. In 1864, General Phineas Banning built a Greek Revival house for his family in Wilmington, California, that reflects its locale in its use of redwood timbers for the frame.

Greek Revival architecture continues to exert its influence today. In fact, one of the most read-about new houses in America is a contemporary interpretation of this classical style. It is the house that *House* is all about. The best-selling book by Tracy Kidder chronicles the entire process of building a new Greek Revival structure designed by architect William Rawn.

Unlike Greek Revival houses of the nineteenth century, this late twentieth-century interpretation is enlivened with an asymmetric porch on the temple-like wall. The classical columns also have been rendered in a decidedly non-classical way. Instead of being freestanding shafts, they are stylized as decorative pilasters

Throughout the house an abundance of windows brightens the interior. Changing floor levels reinforce the separation of living spaces.

In keeping with modern space-planning tenets, the interior is arranged in an open plan. For example, low work-counters deftly separate the work and the informal eating areas in the kitchen.

attached to the corners of the façade. The arrangement of windows on the side walls reflects the placement and function of each room rather than the classical ideal of visual balance.

The windows also bring a panorama of views directly indoors, particularly in the open-plan living-dining room. The design of the kitchen stresses smooth functioning with a contemporary L-shape work center and an expanse of cabinetry and work space along the opposite wall. Here, classical detailing is brought indoors in the form of cornices atop the upper cabinetry.

The rich tradition of Greek Revival architecture was drawn upon in an entirely different way by architects Simon Ungers and Laszlo Kiss of UKZ in Ithaca, New York, in their design of a weekend retreat for one of their Cornell University architecture professors, Robert Hobbs. Built into a hillside overlooking a lake, this house turns the classical tradition on its head. The base, which usually is nothing more than a utilitarian platform for the building, has been over-scaled to become the actual living space.

The obligatory classical columns have been relocated and given new duties. Instead of supporting the roof, in this version they are set in the base in the form of towering, narrow windows. The gable roof that gives the style its distinct look is rendered abstractly to serve as a rooftop porch with a view.

COTTAGE

Architect Lester Walker's house shows the charm of the American cottage.

Double-height rooms and open areas make the house seem bigger.

Though a cottage is one of those types of houses that seems to be everywhere, people still have a hard time describing exactly what it is. Admittedly imprecise, the term *cottage* can mean anything from an elaborate vacation structure similar to the large camps in the Adirondack Mountains to a cabin, a lodge, or—as anyone who has bought a "handy-man's special" knows—a dump.

In any case, we usually consider a cottage to be any small and unpretentious house in the country or a suburb. Cottages were—and continue to be—built in a number of architectural styles. In New England, they are imbued with the look of the Cape Cod or Saltbox house (see pages 32–35 and 38–39). Cottages built in the West often reflect the stylistic traits of Spanish architecture.

In today's expensive housing market, cottages offer one of the most affordable options to renting. However, older houses of this type can have significant drawbacks: small, cramped rooms, inefficient layouts, and outdated fixtures. As a solution, many families have retained the existing foundation and shell and undertaken remodelings to modernize these houses indoors.

The cottage is not merely an antique house-type. The high cost of residential construction today has prompted many families to turn in desperation to the cottage as their only hope of affording a house. It is also an excellent choice for the design of a weekend or vacation house. Architect and prolific author Lester Walker built such a house in Woodstock, New York. Though it encompasses only 640 square feet of living space, this cottage "lives big" thanks to expanses of glass, built-in cabinetry, and multi-use living areas. The green and blue trim is repeated indoors on vertical elements, making the area seem bigger.

VICTORIAN STYLES

Though we often tend to think of the Victorian Age as monolithic, the architecture and furniture design of the period is as varied as that of any other era. One reason for this unexpected variety is the length of the Victorian Age, which spanned nearly three quarters of the nineteenth century. In England, the Victorian era lasted from the ascendancy of Queen Victoria to the British Throne in 1837 until her death in 1901. In America, the Victorian period began a few years later in 1845, reflecting the time lag in the migration of style from England to the United States.

This period was an era of innovation and revival in architecture and the decorative arts. The Victorian Age began with a revival of the Medieval Gothic style and ended with the emergence of Art Nouveau. In between, a number of historic styles were revived and reinterpreted and new house-types were introduced in architecture: Elizabethan, Italianate, Tuscan, the octagon house, French Second Empire, the Stick and Eastlake styles, Victorian Queen Anne, Richardson Romanesque, Sullivan Romanesque, and the Shingle Style.

In varying degrees, Victorian architectural designs were spread across the country via inexpensive pattern books, the staple medium for disseminating style until the advent of home-decorating magazines. Though standardized in exterior styling and interior layout, Victorian designs were often interpreted in a strictly regional context. The most outstanding examples are the Victorian houses of San Francisco (see pages 118–19). Others achieved their greatest popularity in a specific area such as the Shingle Style, which was overwhelmingly concentrated along the Eastern Seaboard (see pages 42–45).

GOTHIC REVIVAL

A raised foundation gives the Manship House a Southern flavor.

Gothic Revival illustrates how an historic architectural form can be revived and adapted for another time and place. To most of us, Gothic architecture is associated with the great churches of Medieval Britain that were built between the twelfth and fifteenth centuries. In the 1700s and again in the 1800s the style was adapted in America, where fine examples of this architectural genre were built in such diverse areas as the Maryland Tidewater and the deltas of the Mississippi.

Gothic Revival houses built in the nineteenth century are characterized by delicate wood tracery—or gingerbread—and a pointed arch on the gable roof, which was often repeated in the shape of the windows. The style also can be identified by the use of uniform materials, high massive chimneys, and monochromatic color schemes in subdued natural tones to link the house with the site.

An excellent example of the Gothic Revival style that includes distinctive regional elements is the Manship House in Jackson, Mississippi. Most likely, it was inspired by a design in a pattern book, *Architecture of Country Houses*. The basic plan was adapted for the hot southern climate by incorporating traditional cooling methods: a central hall to provide flow-through ventilation and

Architect Hugh Newell Jacobsen pared down the Gothic Revival silhouette for a contemporary look.

Indoors, the towering living area is brightened by geometric cutouts.

floor-to-ceiling windows to promote cross-ventilation. The structure is administered by the Mississippi Department of Archives and History and is open for public tours.

In designing a new house on the Eastern Shore of Maryland, architect Hugh Newell Jacobsen of Washington, D.C. adapted the traditional Tidewater type of Gothic Revival house to meet contemporary needs. Though rendered in a highly stylized manner, the house embodies the characteristics of Gothic Revival architecture. However, Jacobsen flattened the traditional arched window into a contemporary geometric rectangle. The delicate wood tracery, which gave nineteenth-century Gothic Revival houses much of their visual impact, was eliminated in the streamlining.

Indoors, Jacobsen created the impression of a Gothic church while adhering to the tenets of modern space-planning. In the living room, the ceiling soars up to the roof peak creating an airy, spacious volume reminiscent of a cathedral. Otherwise, the interior bears the balanced look of classicism. Flanking the paired, facing sofas are built-in bookcases and matching fireplaces placed on opposite sides of the room. Reflecting this desire for visual balance is the floor plan. To each side of the core of the house are wings of equal size. One contains the kitchen and dining room; the other, a modern master suite. This sense of classical symmetry marks the most significant departure from Gothic and Gothic Revival architecture, which were asymmetric in form.

VILLA

The era of the Victorian Villa reached its zenith with Olana, the house of landscape artist Frederick Church. Church emblazoned his villa with fanciful, Persian-inspired motifs and bright, High Victorian colors.

For the landed gentry of nineteenth-century America, the rural equivalent of the city town house as a symbol of affluence was the villa, a country residence that was large and, often, pretentious. Perhaps no villa in America is quite as striking as Olana, the Upstate New York home of artist Frederick Church, of the Hudson River valley school of painters.

Designed in 1870 and built to reflect the artist's love of Middle Eastern art, Olana is a Persian-inspired fantasy brought to life. The architecture is an eclectic riot of motifs: bay windows, balconies, towers, and a veranda. The interior is an excellent example of how color can be used to define living spaces. The massive interior volumes are painted in High Victorian colors and detailed with Middle Eastern motifs, painted and stenciled by Church. Olana, located near the town of Hudson, is operated by the New York State Historic Trust and is open for public tours.

Another Victorian villa has also been resurrected by architect James V. Righter of New Haven, Connecticut, who designed a modern version to replace an original example that was destroyed in a fire. The asymmetric house is smaller than the original, but is set at an angle so that the viewer sees two sides at once, making the structure seem much bigger than it is.

To unify the design, Righter specified a uniform exterior of shingles that have been allowed to weather. An abundance of windows arranged as bands recall Victorian houses but are rendered in clearly contemporary solid glass panels. Dormer windows create the impression that the house consists of four stories when actually it only has three. Reminiscent of many Victorian houses, this one centers on the living area, a two-story high room that includes the dining area. Here, Victorian influences give way to the modern in the furnishings—an L-shaped banquette ringed by windows that bring the view indoors.

Olana incorporates an array of architectural details including bay windows and a soaring tower.

Architect James V. Righter deftly updated the classic lines of the Victorian Villa in this new house.

A row of modern sliding glass doors wraps around the exterior illuminating the open-plan public rooms.

NINETEENTH·CENTURY ECLECTICISM

Redwood construction gives the William Carson House regional roots.

This house may not have been the inspiration for Alfred Hitchcock's movie "Psycho," but, unlike most of us, Norman Bates and his mother would have felt right at home here. Victorian architects were famous for borrowing elements from a variety of styles and blending them together in almost salad-bowl fashion to create something entirely original. This practice reached its zenith in the William Carson residence in Eureka, California.

Designed by Samuel and Joseph Newsom and built in 1885, the house embodies every architectural grudge contemporary Americans have against their Victorian ancestors from the drab color scheme to every last overwrought detail. However, the structure represents a regional interpretation in its materials. The entire house is constructed of California redwood, which gives the otherwise placelessness of the architecture regional roots.

Stylistically, the house combines a large covered porch of Victorian Queen Anne architecture, the pointed gables of Gothic Revival, shingle detailing, turrets, and just about every other example of Victorian architectural motifs there is.

ROMANESQUE

While Victorian eclecticism was running riot across the land, architects were reviving the forms and motifs of the buildings of Medieval western and southern Europe. Inherently simple and utilitarian, these forms were reinterpeted for late Victorian life as a revolt against the excesses of the High Victorian years.

The master of the Romanesque Revival, as it was called, was architect Henry Hobson Richardson of Boston, and it is by his name that this movement came to be called Richardson Romanesque. His most successful house is the 19,000-square-foot John J. Glessner House in Chicago, which was built between 1875 and 1877. Glessner, a vice-president of the International Harvester

Though large and luxurious for its time, the John J. Glessner House in Chicago was an attempt to return to simpler architectural forms during the High Victorian Age. The small windows protected privacy indoors.

Preserved in mint condition, the study of the Glessner House is an outstanding example of the upper-class taste in the Gilded Age. Beneath a coffered ceiling are huge globe lights, beautiful built-in cabinetry, and a massive fireplace mantel to visually anchor the room.

Company, was also a patron of the arts, who served as a trustee of the Art Institute and the Chicago Orchestral Association.

Composed of stones laid in rows, the Norman-inspired façade resembles multiple layers of geological strata. This rugged exterior is balanced by informal walls facing a rear courtyard. The windows on the front wall are small to add privacy; on the rear wall they are large to frame the view. The Glessner House, credited with being one of the first modern houses in America, was so advanced for its time that curator Elaine Herrington describes the house as avant-garde. Open for public touring, the Glessner House is maintained by the Chicago Architecture Foundation.

A•FRAME

Practically all roof, the A-Frame is the quintessential American vacation house.

Whenever we think of this type of house, images of ski slopes or ocean beaches immediately come to mind. And no wonder, for besides being born in the U.S.A., the A-Frame has become the all-American vacation house. Inexpensive to build and practical for an informal residence, the A-Frame is distinctive in its design— it's practically all roof. Indeed, the steeply pitched gable roof in most cases extends almost to the ground and doubles as the side walls. The front and back are usually simple straight walls cut to meet the angle of the roof.

However, what makes the A-Frame particularly suitable as a vacation house is the interior, which emphasizes communal living space as opposed to private areas such as bedrooms. This de-

sign is based, in part, on the theory that when people are vacationing together, they want to spend more time visiting with one another than engaged in private pursuits. The A-Frame encourages this sort of togetherness.

Generally, the first floor is designated as a communal area consisting of a living-dining area and a kitchen. The ceiling of the living area, and sometimes the dining area, rises to the roofpeak creating the illusion of greater spaciousness. As a rule, the kitchen is placed to the rear beneath a second-floor loft. Often, there is also a bathroom or laundry at the rear. Typically, the second-floor loft serves as the sleeping space and may consist of one larger bedroom or be subdivided into two smaller ones.

AMERICAN POSTMODERN

Nautical motifs enliven this elegant example of Postmodernism by Venturi, Rauch and Scott Brown.

One of the most controversial recent developments in architecture is Postmodernism. It has been called everything from art to nonsense. So exactly what is it? A Postmodern building is a Modern structure that has been enlivened by historical details.

Unlike authentic historical styles, however, the historical motifs incorporated into Postmodern structures are not recreated literally. Instead, historical motifs are twisted and turned, over-scaled, and under-scaled, or executed in wildly untraditional materials. Author Joan Kron put it best in an article she wrote for *Residential Interiors* magazine, describing the style as "a witty brooch of historical illusion pinned on a contemporary ensemble."

Though Postmodernism is still in its infant stage, several ar-

chitects have carved out enviable reputations in this genre or created buildings that best illustrate the style: Michael Graves; Peter Rose of Montreal, Canada; and Graham Gund of Cambridge, Massachusetts. Probably the best known firm to design and build Postmodern houses is the firm of Venturi, Rauch and Scott Brown of Philadelphia.

In a way, Postmodernism shares a common trait with Art Deco architecture—it can either be deadly serious as exemplified by the Chrysler Building in New York City or it can be fanciful, much like the 1930s resort architecture of Miami Beach, where a hotel might be designed in the form of a ship.

The fanciful is more fun. One of the best examples of a fanciful

Modern glazing frames the view while the vaulted ceiling is an historical touch.

Postmodern house is the one in Stony Creek, Connecticut, designed in 1979 by architect Steve Izenour of Venturi, Rauch and Scott Brown with the assistance of Christine Matheu. It was built by Eric Stone and George Izenour between 1980 and 1983.

The site of the house was formerly commercial; it was a granite loading dock until the 1920s and then an oyster dock until the 1960s. The house itself is almost square in the historical bungalow shape. It is elevated for protection against hurricanes and floods and the roof is a simple gable shape. Befitting its seaside location, the house is embellished with a large "rose window" ship wheel on the north-facing facade.

The ship wheel is echoed on the south wall by a window, which overlooks Long Island Sound, that is reminiscent of a Federal fanlight above the door. When viewed from the water, the house resembles an ancient temple with wood steps leading up to the porch. Protecting the interior from bright light is a roof overhang supported by four highly stylized and flattened out "Doric" columns that serve as a windbreak. The east and west walls have a diagonal design of white, while scalloped shingles evoke the feeling of Victorian all-over patterning. The cedar shingles and trim have been left to weather naturally to a silver-gray.

Visitors enter through a vestibule that opens around a fire-

The vault motif reappears in the living area where it conceals sound equipment.

place into the 35-foot-long living room with a vaulted ceiling that rises to a height of 27 feet. This breathtaking room is rich in imagery. While the intricately patterned vault recalls Middle Eastern splendor, it is also practical; it is made of strips of wood backed with theatrical scrim (durable, loosely woven cotton or linen fabric) to conceal stereo speakers and video equipment. Cathode-ray tubing, radiating a cool light, is tucked behind the upper rim.

Two sets of sliding glass doors and two large windows bring the sweeping view of Long Island Sound into the opposite end of the room. Here, the fanlight illuminates the vault and emphasizes the curve of the ceiling.

Stripped of its Postmodern motifs, the house is a complex structure organized in a thoroughly modern manner. For example, the center stairwell buffers noise between the master bedroom and the living room. And to protect the owner's privacy from neighbors nearby, the west wall has only a few windows. This house has received many awards for its excellence: It was named a "Record House" by *Architectural Record,* a leading professional journal; received a Silver Award from the Philadelphia chapter of the American Institute of Architects; a First award from the Red Cedar Shingle and Handsplit Shake Bureau; and an honor award from the American Wood Council.

ENERGY■EFFICIENT ARCHITECTURE

Angled to the south, this passive solar house soaks up the sun and its heat on even the coldest clear days. A fireplace provides more warmth while heavy insulation reduces heat loss to the outdoors.

While some architects are moving beyond Modernism into Postmodernism, others are headed in an entirely different direction. Their destination is not stylistic art but practical living. This movement manifests itself in the development of the energy-efficient house. While the Postmodernists were looking for style, architects interested in energy efficiency were seeking alternatives to high utility bills and an unhealthy dependency on a fossil fuel supply controlled by foreign interests.

Heating and cooling by mechanical means is so universal in the United States that many of us tend to forget they are a product of twentieth-century technology. So when foreign countries turned off the fuel that made the technology work, the question naturally arose, "How did Americans heat and cool their houses before central air conditioning?"

Architects have put lessons learned from historical building techniques to good use in the past decade. Because these techniques are practical products of the past, they mesh seamlessly with many historic house-types. In addition, the contemporary look created by extensive use of glass to capture the heat of the sun enables them to blend into Modern architecture.

So exactly what is an energy-efficient house and how does it work? While there are several variations—the super-insulated, envelope, and the photo-voltaic house to name only three—the type that has most successfully gained public acceptance is the solar house. This type of architecture falls into two categories—the active and the passive systems.

Active solar systems use groups of glass-faced boxes called solar panels to absorb solar heat. Generally, these panels are set on the south-facing portion of the roof where they receive the most sunlight. The heat gained by the panels is absorbed by either water or air, which is then pumped by mechanical equipment to a storage area. In liquid systems, the water runs through pipes to a heat-storage tank that looks much like a conventional hot water heater. Storage in air-based systems is usually provided by a basement bin filled with rocks. When the stored heat is needed to warm the living areas, it is circulated through conventional duct work into the different areas of the house.

Because the active system requires mechanical equipment to transfer heat, it has yielded in popularity to the passive-solar system. However, active systems continue to be utilized for specific purposes such as heating the domestic water supply.

In contrast, the passive-solar system is virtually maintenance free and requires no gadgetry. An expanse of glass on the south-facing wall of the house absorbs the heat of the sun on cold but bright winter days. This heat flows through the living spaces, warming them directly. Extra heat is absorbed by what is called a "thermal mass," usually a concrete floor several inches thick. The thermal mass stores the solar heat until evening (or cloudy days) then releases it gradually to warm the living spaces.

To enhance the aesthetic appeal of the thermal slab without reducing its effectiveness, it is usually disguised with a layer of

Solar heat streaming into a south-facing sunspace via skylights and sliding glass patio doors is stored in a thick, thermal-mass floor.

ceramic tile compatible with the overall color scheme of the house. Instead of a thermal-mass floor, some passive systems store solar heat in a specially built wall of thick masonry called a "Trombe wall." It can be disguised by a layer of ordinary plaster without sacrificing its heat-absorbing ability. Still other systems use large, clear, acrylic containers filled with water to store heat.

In summer, when the sun is higher in the sky, an exterior roof overhang or other shading device prevents sunlight from entering the interior. The windows or sliding glass doors that admit solar

gain in winter can be opened for ventilation. Interior heat is often ventilated outdoors through operable skylights. Two-story houses often incorporate an open stairwell that provides a pathway for lighter-weight hot air to rise to the skylights on the second floor.

The interior is arranged in an open plan so that warm and cool air circulate freely and evenly through the various rooms. The living area and, often, the dining area and kitchen are placed along the south wall. This assures that they will be heated via direct gain during the day and be comfortably warm for family gatherings in the evening. This arrangement also enables these areas to take advantage of the outdoor view through the glazing. Bedrooms generally are along the colder north wall along with other spaces such as closets, utility rooms, the laundry, and bathrooms that need less heat. North-facing entrances have double doorways creating an airlock that reduces heat loss to the outdoors when they are opened and closed.

Passive-solar technology is most efficient when it is incorporated into the overall architecture of a new house. Sometimes an interior space, such as the living area, doubles as the heat-gathering mechanism. More often, new houses are designed to include a sunroom or greenhouse that serves the same purpose yet can be closed off in summer to keep unwanted heat out of the envelope of the house. Many older houses can benefit to varying degrees by being retrofitted with the addition of a heat-gathering mechanism such as a sunroom or greenhouse.

It is important to understand that the technology is not a magical cure for high utility costs. Many older houses with little southern exposure cannot be retrofitted at all. Even in new houses, a passive-solar system can rarely supply even half of the space heating, although it can greatly reduce fuel bills. (Lending institutions almost always require the installation of a mechanical system to obtain a building loan.) Badly designed passive systems are a nightmare. They are plagued by searing glare from sunlight throughout the year, excessive and insufficient heating in different areas of the house in winter, and in warm weather by poor ventilation that can send air conditioning bills skyrocketing.

In this outstanding example of a contemporary solar house, the heat-harvesting glazing is incorporated directly into the architectural shell of the structure rather than standing out as an auxiliary sunspace.

FURNISHINGS AND OBJECTS

PART

III

CHAPTER

NINE

The furniture of the Northeast is among the most desirable of all of the American decorative arts. The Colonial tradition is considered *the* quintessential American furniture style in the minds of many. In recent years, the furniture designs of the Shakers have enjoyed a wildly successful revival. The rustic furnishings associated with the Adirondack or Camp style of architecture are popular for the outdoors and, increasingly, indoors. Folk art and furnishings have soared in acceptability with outstanding examples being collected and preserved by museums and reproduced by major manufacturers.

In addition, the Northeast generated some of the finest examples of American interpretations of furniture styles derived from European sources, primarily England. Such historic styles as Chippendale and Hepplewhite, among many others, play a significant role in the furnishings of the Northeast.

These furnishings—the high-style and the more rustic— fit seamlessly into many historic house-types. They are equally appropriate for modern houses where their natural materials, such as wood and textiles unadulterated by manmade fibers, strike a note of contrast and visually add warmth to the spare lines of many modern buildings.

Older than America, the Windsor chair blends seamlessly into traditional decor.

THE COLONIAL TRADITION

Dating from colonial days, the Paul Revere bowl may be one of the most popular designs in America.

The furniture designs of Colonial America have captured the public imagination time and time again. Colonial furnishings have been avidly collected by private individuals and notable museums including the Metropolitan Museum of Art, Concord Antiquarian Museum, Fruitlands Museum, Congress Hall, Shelburne Museum, and Wadsworth Atheneum. At well-known auction houses such as Sotheby's and Christie's, top-quality pieces of American Colonial furniture frequently bring thousands of dollars.

In today's home furnishings market, the term "Colonial" is elastic. It is used to describe a variety of styles from Jacobean and William and Mary to Federal, a time span of nearly 200 years. Many pieces simply defy such classification altogether. What they all have in common, however, is simplicity. They are the furnishings of necessity, not art. Even so, the spare, clean lines of Colonial furnishings—and their modern interpretations—imbue them with an artfulness that appeals to many contemporary Americans.

INTERPRETATIONS OF ENGLISH FURNITURE STYLES

The artifacts of the colonial era have been gracefully blended in an artful vignette. Modern-day applications of old-time details include the weathervane as a decorative accessory. The cabinetry adds a lovely rustic touch.

America has a rich tradition of regional furnishings. Historic furnishings associated with a specific region are being made today by individual craftspeople using, in many cases, original tools and techniques. A number of mass manufacturers have picked up on the trend and are offering collections of regional furnishings, often under licensing agreements with museums and historic preservation groups. These range from line-for-line reproductions and adaptations of older designs to Postmodern pieces "inspired by" regional historicism.

As is the case today, many furnishings trends exert themselves all at once. Such was the case in colonial-era America. On one level was the more rustic colonial furniture. At the other end of the scale were the American versions of formal English styles. The result is a treasure trove of American decorative arts and the furniture that most often comes to mind when we think of traditional decorating.

QUEEN ANNE

Uniquely American, the highboy reached maturity as a furniture design during the Queen Anne period.

Characterized by a curving, or cabriole, leg, the Queen Anne style was popular during an era of important cultural changes that effected the design of furniture. For example, in the 1730s drinking tea became fashionable, spurring the development of the tea table. The most popular form of the tea table, both in New England and as far south as New York City, was rectangular. Another innovation was the invention of the folding-top card table, and the evolution of a uniquely American high chest—or highboy—with large, carved shells on the drawers and a scrolled pediment.

Prominent cabinetmakers worked along the Eastern Seaboard from Boston to Philadelphia. Because of differences in the furniture made in each of these areas, it is often possible to determine where a specific piece of furniture was made. Some of the finest examples of the Queen Anne style originated in Philadelphia. Here, a typical Queen Anne chair incorporated web and pad feet, a seat in the shape of a horseshoe, a scrolled splat (slat of wood in the middle of a chair back), and concave arms.

Spare proportions, delicate shapes, and slender chair legs

This vivid, unabashedly Postmodern version of the Queen Anne chair was designed by architect Robert Venturi.

are the earmarks of Queen Anne furniture that was made in Massachusetts. The cabinetmakers of Newport, Rhode Island, imbued their Queen Anne designs with the famous claw-and-ball foot, the silhouette of a shell on the crest rail of chairs, and narrow splats. Their favored material during the Queen Anne period was dark mahogany. Craftsmen in New York also carved the claw-and-ball foot but theirs generally was more square.

An interesting development in the design of historically inspired furniture mirrors a common practice in architecture today.

Many old houses without significant historical value are restored on the exterior and remodeled indoors into an open floor plan with multifunctional spaces rather than distinct rooms for specific activities such as dining, entertaining, and reading. In furniture design, many historic forms are adapted for today's home furnishings market in much the same way. The result is a piece of furniture that reflects the historic shapes and lines of its stylistic predecessor. It is important to remember that these are not Queen Anne furnishings, merely modern furniture designed in that style.

CHIPPENDALE

Dominant between the years of 1755 and 1790, the Chippendale style developed during a period of great political unrest that culminated in the writing of the Declaration of Independence and the War of Independence with England. Despite the turmoil, architecture and design flourished. Buildings and furniture of the period are characterized by a great many influences, many of them international. Designs based on the work of the Italian Renaissance architect Andrea Palladio were translated by American carpenters into buildings. Indoors, these houses were often decorated with compatible motifs including wallpaper painted with scenes of Roman ruins.

These are the houses for which Chippendale furniture was made. Chippendale has come to mean not only the furniture designed and made by the English cabinetmaker Thomas Chippendale but the many Chippendalelike copies and adaptations.

Queen Anne details such as the scrolled splat distinguish American Chippendale furnishings.

A modern Chippendale-style chair retains the serpentine back.

American interpretations of Chippendale furniture differ significantly from the English originals. English Chippendale furniture embodies a variety of different motifs—Gothic, Chinese, and Rococo. American Chippendale furniture, on the other hand, is more traditional and incorporates a number of Queen Anne details. This makes the American version of Chippendale virtually unique.

For example, an American Chippendale armchair can be identified by its Queen Anne scrolled splat, concave arms, and ball-and-claw foot. The American Chippendale highboy usually has a Queen Anne scrolled pediment and shell-carved drawers. Also uniquely American is the practice of Newport craftsmen, such as the related families of Goddard and Townsend, who combined shell carvings and blockfront construction. This type of design has two vertical rectangles flanking a recessed rectangle. Shells decorate the top and bottom of the rectangles.

The Chippendale era was a time of new furniture innovations for America such as the introduction of the Pembroke table, a form of the drop-leaf table frequently used for eating breakfast; the breakfront, a bookcase consisting of a cabinet above an enclosed section (and often a center section that extends outward); and the sofa, which was derived from the settee. The most famous variety of the Chippendale sofa has a serpentine back with rolled arms. The rectangular Queen Anne tea table evolved into a "gallery-top china table" with a pierced or raised edge. Though the tripod tea table was known in America during the Queen Anne era, it became fully developed during the Chippendale period.

THE CLASSICAL PERIOD

Roman Classicism is inherent in Hepplewhite furniture.

The American Revolution ended America's political dependency on England. Northeastern cabinetmakers, however, continued copying and adapting the furniture styles of England and other European countries, notably France. The Classical Period of 1790 to 1830 embraced a number of familiar styles—Hepplewhite (1790–1810), Sheraton (1800–1810), and Empire (1810–1820) including Late Sheraton (1815–1820) and Late Empire (1820–1830).

Beginning about 1790, a wave of classicism swept through European culture, primarily resulting from archaeological discoveries in the ruins of two Roman cities, Herculaneum in the early 1700s and Pompeii in 1749. The foremost interpreter of classical design in England was Robert Adam. In America, two men shared the title—George Hepplewhite (?–1786) and Thomas Sheraton (1751–1806).

Hepplewhite furniture illustrates the impact of the classical revival on American furniture design. Notable characteristics of Hepplewhite furniture are straight, tapering legs and inlaid decoration. Chair backs are usually oval, heart-shaped, or shieldlike. Sheraton furniture shares many of these characteristics, as the two styles sprang from the same design source.

FOLK FURNITURE

While eras in design have always been labeled by their high-style furniture, there flourishes a less sophisticated form known as folk furniture. A European tradition, folk furniture can best be described as pieces made by the neighborhood cabinetmaker for local villagers. Furniture of this genre was made for the less affluent and was found in many lower- and middle-class families. Folk art was transplanted by European immigrants who continued the tradition in America.

Folk furnishings became an area of serious study by the historians of the decorative arts in the 1920s. One of the great repositories of fine examples of the genre is the Museum of American Folk Art in New York City. The museum has an impressive permanent collection of quilts and other furnishings. In addition, it has access to exceptional art items in private collections that are often exhibited, both in its New York City museum and sometimes in traveling shows.

Interior designers today usually choose furniture in a much more relaxed manner than in the past. While in the past furnishings of a single style were selected, now an important trend is to blend furniture of diverse styles—Continental and American, old and new—that reflect the spirit of eclecticism that has become the dominant style of our time.

THE WINDSOR CHAIR

The Windsor chair remains one of the most popular folk designs.

One of the best-known examples of early folk furniture, the Windsor chair originated, not surprisingly, in England. Common in England and in the American colonies in the eighteenth century, this chair has a spindle back and legs that slant outward. The Windsor chair was made in six different varieties: comb-back, fan-back, loop-back, low-back, bow-back, and the New England armchair. The New England Windsor was altered to include a shelf and a drawer combining the requirements of a chair and a desk in one piece of furniture. Windsor chairs usually were constructed of unseasoned wood—pine, maple, ash, chestnut, or birch.

SHAKER FURNITURE

The Windsor chairs and trestle table evoke a range of images—from the difficult times of the eighteenth century when furnishings were handmade to the colonial era and the Shakers. These furnishings represent the work of the Shakers, who lived in self-contained communities.

Shaker furnishings and architecture blend seamlessly in a room at Shaker Village. Because of its spare, clean lines, Shaker furniture is particularly popular today.

The Shaker religious movement was founded by Mother Ann Lee, who with eight adherents emigrated from England to the United States in 1774. The official name of the sect was "The United Society of Believers in Christ's Second Appearing" but because of the shaking dance that was part of their religious ritual, members were called "Shakers" by the public.

The Shakers have been best described in a painstakingly researched book, *The American Shakers and Their Furniture,* by John G. Shea. He relates that Shakers equated physical labor with worship and were organized into working communities. Though the Shaker life was strict—they vowed self-denial, including celibacy —the movement grew until the mid-1800s. Then, at its peak, the Shakers had some eighteen communities and 6000 adherents.

The Shakers' furniture is a testament to their skill in design and construction. The pieces are plain, spare, and free of decorative frills. Chair and table legs are tapered and the joinery is

The Shakers' ladder-back chair is a sophisticated blend of exposed joinery and the texture of a handwoven seat with delicately tapered legs.

exposed. To show the beauty of the wood veneers were left off.

The archetypal Shaker chair is a standard ladder-back. The seats were made by the women members of the sect using either a woven tape or rush. The Shakers also used built-in furniture, primarily chests. Beds were little more than cots. It is this simplicity and no-nonsense design that has made Shaker furniture particularly popular in this age of Modernism. Unlike Modern furniture, however, the pieces are made of warm wood and natural fibers that enable them to fit into today's clean-lined houses.

Examples of Shaker furniture are in the permanent collections of many museums—The Shaker Museum in Old Chatham, New York; Hancock Shaker Village, Hancock, Massachusetts; The Museum of Folk American Art, New York City; the Fruitlands Museum, Cambridge, Massachusetts; and the Henry Ford Museum, Dearborn, Michigan. A number of reproduction pieces are manufactured for sale in completed form or as kits.

RUSTIC FURNITURE

The Adirondack chair is one of the most popular types of rustic furniture around.

The emergence of the great camps of the Adirondack Mountains in upstate New York (see pages 62–65) inspired an entire new genre of furnishings—the Rustic Style. The name, however, is in part a misnomer. While the pieces were unmistakably rustic in design, especially when compared to mainstream styles of the same periods, the craftsmanship involved in making these pieces lends them an artfulness that makes rustic furniture a favorite of collectors. Rustic is a catch-all designation covering several types from Adirondack Style to bentwillow, and twig and bark furniture.

Many of these were made by individual craftsmen who were employed on great estates or who had wealthy patrons. As the popularity of rustic furnishings grew, however, manufacturers joined in making pieces for the mass market. Indeed, much of their output found its way into the Adirondack camps themselves. One of the best known manufacturers was the Hickory Chair Company, whose 1922 product catalogue listed more than 100 items including a small dining chair for $4.25 and an entire summer house measuring twelve feet in diameter for $300.

Today, rustic furniture is popular once again. They are made in a wide variety of styles by individual craftsmen such as Daniel Mack of New York City as well as specialty manufacturers including Lodgepole Furniture of Jackson, Wyoming, Weatherend Estate Furniture of Rockland, Maine, Willsboro Wood Products of Boston, and Grant's of Lake Placid, New York.

CHAPTER

TEN ■

Regional interpretations of high styles can be found in the formal furniture of Charleston, which was a center of Southern design in the eighteenth century, as well as on the rural plantations where furniture, though more rustic, was of high-quality construction and intriguing design. Not only are there regional translations of traditional English styles—the backbone of American design through the nineteenth century—but the vibrant influences of French design are also prevalent.

This region of the country has proven to be rich in design inspiration for today's manufacturers. Several are engaged in manufacturing programs in which they are licensed by historical groups to make authorized reproductions and what are called adaptations of original museum-quality furnishings, some of which still grace private houses. Colonial Williamsburg, for example, has one of the largest and oldest such licensing programs that includes wallpapers, fabrics, accessories to dinnerware, crystal, silver, and pewter, in addition to furniture.

The airiness and light coloring of this interior show a reliance on the traditional elements of Southern design.

INTERPRETATIONS OF ENGLISH FURNITURE STYLES

Regional furniture spans the range of style from high to humble. The designs of high-style furnishings, as a rule, reflect the influence of the prevailing fashion in decorating at any given time. Many of these diverse styles were watered down for mass consumption. Historically, American furnishings have generally followed the mainstream English styles. The "Americanization" and, sometimes, "regionalization" that distinguishes them from their European counterparts frequently is their simpler design. Generally, American furniture is more vertical and less square. Carving, particularly on chairs, is less pronounced.

Just as the cabinetmakers of the Northeast looked to England for design trends, so too did their counterparts in the South. Unlike the cabinetmakers of the North, however, those in the South had only one great furniture-making center until after the American Revolution—Charleston, South Carolina. And it is the houses of this city that provide some of the finest Southern examples of high-style English furnishings.

CHARLESTON FURNITURE

The furnishings of old Charleston are faithfully reproduced by Baker.

Because of the city's prosperity in the eighteenth century as a flourishing center of trade, Charleston furniture is much closer in design to the original English designs than that of the Northeast. Nevertheless, the furniture made in the city bears unique regional characteristics. An excellent example is the secretary-bookcase, also called a chest-on-chest. As Helen Comstock points out in *American Furniture*, the Charleston chest-on-chest can be identified by the flat top over a fret-carved frieze. The incorporation of fretwork in the design was popularized by the city's outstanding cabinetmaker of the eighteenth-century, Thomas Elfe. The motif

became known as the "Elfe fret" even when used by other cabinetmakers. Rice fronds also were carved on the posts of the famous "Rice Bed," in honor of the city's major import, rice. The favored material for Charleston furniture of the eighteenth century was mahogany that was imported from the Caribbean.

Unfortunately, much of the furniture from eighteenth-century Charleston has been destroyed over the years. However, many of the pieces that have survived have been reproduced for today's market by Baker Furniture Company in several styles including Queen Anne and Chippendale.

Renditions of rice fronds embellish a reproduction of the eighteenth-century "Rice Bed," one of the most famous of Charleston's regional designs. Like the original, this one is made of imported mahogany.

PLANTATION FURNITURE

A reproduction of the plantation version of the Chippendale settee retains the classic serpentine back.

In the rural South, owners of vast tobacco plantations imported many fine examples of English furniture. To these, they added pieces made by American craftsmen. Like the Charleston furniture, plantation pieces were designed and constructed in the prevalent style of the time—from Queen Anne to Chippendale and Hepplewhite—but are generally simpler, though not rustic. Since 1911, prominent pieces of furniture from the plantations of Virginia have been reproduced by the Hickory Chair Company.

A reproduction of a plantation mirror embodies the classical lines and detailing associated with eighteenth-century design and architecture.

FRENCH INFLUENCES

The Bolduc House retains a few precious pieces of rustic Arcadian furniture.

Beginning about 1810, high-style American furniture reflected the impact of French design as seen in the work of Duncan Phyfe. His work was influenced by the English Regency style, which itself was based on the French Directoire style.

On another level, the impact of historic French furniture forms was more direct. This is especially true for furniture made in the South in the early nineteenth century. The Arcadians who migrated down the Mississippi River from Canada to Louisiana brought along their furniture designs as well as their architecture.

While the furniture of the major cities of America—Charleston, New York, Philadelphia, Newport, and Boston, among others—was extremely sophisticated, Arcadian pieces were more rustic. In addition, many of the designs were quite old, dating from the seventeenth century. Throughout the nineteenth century, these forms were copied and gradually updated to incorporate Victorian Age innovations such as the comfort of upholstered seating.

FOLK TRADITION

Isolated in rural areas, Southerners twisted twigs and tree branches into beautiful furniture.

Throughout the South, but particularly in Appalachia, the only furniture early settlers had was that which they could make. Akin to the furnishings of the Rustic Style popularized in the Adirondacks (see page 173), the folk furnishings of the South are unabashedly rustic. The materials they incorporate are those found at hand—twigs and tree branches—that are fabricated in a straightforward, no-nonsense manner.

Though they are unmistakably utilitarian in their appearance, the furnishings of the folk tradition reflect an imaginative approach to design. It requires quite a sense of inventiveness to twist and turn twigs and tree branches into chairs and tables that are witty, and always functional.

Some surviving examples of Southern folk furniture are surprisingly artful, with sculptural curves and decorative embellish-

An array of stretchers and back rails characterize the Southern ladder-back chair.

ments. The design of the rocking chair—a staple of Southern front porch comfort—was pared down to the essentials necessary for structural support. However, even these display a bit of wit, with rings of bent wood that add a decorative touch while serving as armrests. Some designs are even sparer and dispense with armrests altogether. The visual effect for the viewer is literally that of a chair on rockers.

Many pieces are imbued with the simplicity that became a hallmark of Shaker design. The southern translation of the Shaker approach resulted in chairs with slightly flared backs, a profusion of stretchers for proper support, and delicately tapered legs. Handicrafts were essential to many pieces. A variety of natural materials, which were woven into seats, visually soften the strict geometry of the overall design.

CHAPTER
ELEVEN ■

The Southwest is the undiscovered treasure trove of American regional furnishings. Besides the obvious Wild West motifs that were seen by anyone who spent a Saturday morning in front of the television set in the 1950s, the Southwest has a proud multi-national tradition of decorative arts.

The Hispanic influence is readily seen in the leather uphol-stered seating and beautifully carved woodwork in the houses of New Mexico. European styles are represented, too, in Texas where settlers from northwest Germany brought with them the Biedermeier style of the nineteenth century. Some examples of their craftsmanship is as exacting as that found in the Continental European renditions of the style. Others are less sophisticated yet beautiful interpretations that reflect a freshness and vitality that comes from executing a stately European design style in pine, one of the preeminent materials for southwestern furniture.

In addition, the Southwest has one of the largest concentra-tions of craftsmen and women in the country. The decorative arts they are producing are not only appealing in their design but se-ductive in their appropriateness and fidelity to a sometimes strange—yet wonderful—part of America.

In a modern adobe house, the living room centers around a fire-place handsculpted from stucco.

HISPANIC INFLUENCES

Raised panels and simple metal hinges reflect Hispanic influences on this modern armoire made by Lane for the Museum of American Folk Art.

A number of furniture forms were introduced to the Southwest by the Spanish and, later, the Mexican settlers during the colonial period. Local craftsmen modified these forms for local conditions and needs while retaining much of the original Hispanic detailing.

Rendered in a simpler fashion than their Spanish or Mexican prototypes, southwestern furniture is streamlined and fully in tune with today's aesthetic. For example, cabinet doors are secured by iron hinges that were hand-forged with utility rather than decoration in mind. Yet the woodwork bears the stamp of its Hispanic origins in its decorative motifs that include stylized sunbursts, raised carving, and "rope twist" legs on tables. In addition, craftsmen took full advantage of regional materials such as durable leather to cover and, thus, protect fragile wood tabletops.

Designs that were popular in the Southwest in the nineteenth century were based on those found in Spain 100 years earlier illustrating the time-lag in the communication of style from the Old World to the New. Favored shapes were stark squares and rectangles, which were visually softened by a series of indentations that are carved—sometimes in a "stepped" design—on the sides. These give the pieces a classical air that blends with the Hispanic motifs to create a unique Southwest look.

INTERPRETATIONS OF EUROPEAN STYLES

The clean, geometric lines of the German Biedermeier style can be seen readily in this reproduction armoire constructed of pine.

In the 1840s, political upheavals in continental Europe generated a wave of immigration to America. Many of those immigrants were Germans who settled in the Midwest and Southwest. Texas was a favored destination for many of these new Americans and they tended to concentrate around Austin in what is known as the Rocky Hill Country.

The Germanic influence is readily seen today in the names of the towns such as Fredericksburg. The jewel of the Texas Hill Country, Fredericksburg is graced with tidy stone houses that vividly illustrate the German tradition of building with masonry as well as the regional tradition of utilizing the materials at hand, in this case stone.

The German craftsmen who settled in Texas included fine masters as well as local cabinetmakers. The legacy of woodwork they have left reflects the range of their woodworking and design skills. One of the favored styles was the classically inspired German Biedermeier, which was prevalent in Texas in the 1850s and 60s. Some are faithfully executed examples of the European style. Others represent simplified versions of the Biedermeier style with the added regional twist of being constructed of pine.

FOLK TRADITION

Many motifs from Hispanic and Germanic traditions were combined in the simple folk furniture that was made in the Southwest. Sometimes, both influences are incorporated into the same piece of furniture. As a result, frontier pine chests can be found that are constructed in classical forms and decorated with carving that is reminiscent of Medieval Spain. More common, however, are

A reproduction settee and cedar chest combines Biedermeier styling with the flat back splats of the Texas folk-furniture tradition.

simple designs that are given an unexpected sense of elegance with delicate tapered legs.

Sometimes, a single piece of furniture represents an amalgamation of design forms. For example, a local Southwest craftsman might combine a seating and a storage unit into one, multifunctional piece of furniture.

Unknown in pioneer days, a modern cocktail table adapts the flat top of Texas pioneer furniture and Biedermeier-derived flared legs.

CONTEMPORARY CRAFTS

The folk tradition of the nineteenth century was set firmly in the realm of what today is called handicrafts. Established on a design tradition very different from mainstream furnishings, contemporary crafts are not the primitive, rustic designs one might associate with the word craft. Many objects that fall into the category of crafts are extremely sophisticated, and exquisitely made of rare and beautiful materials.

The Southwest is a hotbed of crafts. In areas such as Aspen, Colorado, Santa Fe, New Mexico, and Austin, Texas, significant concentrations of craftsmen with regional and national reputations make pieces inspired by regional and historic themes.

In the hands of a sophisticated craftsperson, the ancient form of a trestle table assumes a sculptural look much like that of the popular Parsons table and one fully in keeping with the best of contemporary furniture design. Seating is distilled to the basic elements, creating a form that is artfully abstract in appearance yet eminently practical to use.

This thoroughly modern version of the traditional trestle table by Rena Swentzel takes center stage in her Santa Fe home.

CHAPTER
TWELVE ■

It may come as some surprise that the Midwest has been a center of American furniture design and manufacturing. In fact, between 1870 and 1890, more furniture was made in Chicago than in any other locale in the United States.

The stylistic range of Midwest furniture is equally staggering. The great bulk of the Midwest's prodigious output of furniture was made by mass production in any number of styles commonly found across America in the nineteenth century. Yet even many of these are firmly rooted in the Midwest in their materials. Much more interesting, however, are the furnishings that personify regional design aesthetics.

In the case of the Midwest, those aesthetics are of the Arts and Crafts Movement as well as the Prairie School. Both of these greatly influenced interior design throughout the region and, indeed, throughout the country.

A room in the Metropolitan Museum of Art preserves the custom furnishings of Frank Lloyd Wright in their original setting.

ARTS AND CRAFTS MOVEMENT

In a remodeled house, a new trestle-legged table and chairs fashioned by David Frisk of San Diego keep alive the Arts and Crafts tradition. The theme is reinforced by the light fixture of German glass overhead.

The Minneapolis Handicraft Guild produced this lovely, beaten-copper jardiniere.

This design aesthetic was pioneered in England and reached the United States during the last quarter of the nineteenth century. Unique to the English-speaking world, the Arts and Crafts Movement grew out of discontent with the excesses of High Victorian furniture, whose designs were caricatures of French and Italian pieces and, for the most part, were poorly constructed and burdened with excessive amounts of machine-carved decoration. A number of English designers looked to the past for inspiration. They found that in the Gothic style and in the exacting hand-craftsmanship of the Middle Ages. Thus was born the Arts and Crafts Movement, which stressed the handmaking of sturdy, simply designed furnishings.

The Arts and Crafts Movement was not so much a style as

an attitude. In England, it was rooted in the desire for social reform—raising the crafting of furniture to the level of art and giving the artisans that created it a sense of dignity. In short, it was a revolt against the machine and the Industrial Revolution. The movement was led in England by William Morris as well as by a number of architects including C. F. A. Voysey, Charles Rennie Mackintosh, and Charles Eastlake.

In the United States, the Arts and Crafts Movement was less socially minded as the machine was more welcome in a country with a less populous labor force. It was championed by influential designers such as Gustav Stickley, who is remembered for his Mission-Style furniture, and Elbert Hubbard. In both countries, however, leading proponents tended to view the architecture and

Though new, this Mission-Style hanging light fixture manufactured by Rejuvenation House Parts is a faithful reproduction of the original.

interior design as a whole. As a result, many examples of Arts and Crafts furnishings have strong architectural lines and very little decorative embellishment.

It is important to remember that the furniture of the Arts and Crafts Movement represented high style—and high prices. Because intensive hand-labor and fine materials are expensive, it was not furniture for the masses but for the financially elite, who were the patrons of the style. As a result, the output of the Arts and Crafts Movement never flourished on a mass level.

However, the movement did achieve two major triumphs. First, it garnered an impressive number of adherents and, second, it exerted a large influence on another architectural style to come out of the Midwest—the Prairie School. Some notable Arts and Crafts designers were associated with the Prairie School such as George Grant Elmslie, who worked with Frank Lloyd Wright.

The new aesthetic appealed to a segment of the American public, and soon craftsmen's community workshops were established in several parts of the country, one of the largest of which was in Chicago. The movement's philosophy was spread by several publications including *The Craftsman,* a monthly magazine begun by Stickley. It included articles on furniture, decorating, and architecture. Other publications were devoted to providing step-by-step instructions for making Craftsman furniture. Popular between 1900 and 1916, the Mission-Style furniture by Stickley was made of oak fashioned into plain and rectilinear shapes.

The New York City manufacturer Christian Herter contributed beautiful furniture that often incorporated Oriental details. Hubbard worked with a group in East Aurora, New York, called The Roycrofters, which ran a full-fledged community that included many craftsmen, a system of apprentices, and published a magazine called *The Philistine.* The interior design ideas of another enthusiastic backer of the movement, a typographer named Will H. Bradley, were published early in the twentieth century in the *Ladies Home Journal.*

As David M. Cathers points out in his informative and exhaustively researched book *Furniture of the American Arts and Crafts Movement,* contemporary appreciation of Mission-Style furniture began in 1970. That year, the Metropolitan Museum of Art in New York City mounted an exhibition of nineteenth-century American furniture that included a few examples of the Mission Style. Then, in 1972, Robert Judson organized an exhibition for Princeton University that focused on the Arts and Crafts Movement. Wise collectors have been seeking out fine examples of the style ever since.

The popularity of Mission-Style furnishings has spawned several reproduction programs, notably Rejuvenation House Parts of Portland, Oregon. This company offers an array of faithfully reproduced Mission-Style lighting fixtures that have been incorporated into a number of historic restoration projects including the Old Executive Office Building in Washington, D.C., and the State Capitol in Harrisburg, Pennsylvania.

PRAIRIE SCHOOL

Furniture Designed by Architects, Marian Page writes, "Prairie school furniture was as much a part of the architecture that gives it its name as its low hovering roof, its sophisticated spatial arrangements, its strong horizontality. . . . The Prairie school philosophy embraced the idea that every facet of their buildings should contribute to the whole environment—from chairs and tables to lighting and landscaping."

George Grant Elmslie and William Purcell designed this end table.

Harmony of architecture and furnishings was also a hallmark of the Prairie School. Its most well known proponent, Frank Lloyd Wright, was in tune with many of the ideals of the Arts and Crafts Movement. However, while the English members of the movement saw the goal of simplicity in the Gothic forms of the Middle Ages, members of the Prairie School were looking for something altogether new. In fact, Wright even called the contemporary Victorian furnishings of his time "the old order." Ever pragmatic, he saw the machine as a permanent fixture of the new industrial American society. His solution was to come to terms with the machine and use it to society's advantage.

Prairie School furnishings were unprecedented and unrelated to any previous design style for two reasons: the innovative Prairie School house required equally inventive furnishings (see pages 110–13); and the architects of the Prairie School viewed architecture and design as two parts of a single unified whole. In her book,

This billiards chair by George W. Maher is unusual for its massive scale and specialized function. The chair was a small part of Maher's design of a summer house, "Rockridge," in Winona, Minnesota, for E. L. King. This outstanding example of Prairie School furniture is in the collection of the Minnesota Historical Society.

Depending on their clients' budgets, Prairie School architects designed furniture for each of their houses—chairs, tables, benches, desks, cabinets, light fixtures, and sofas. Furnishings were designed with rectilinear lines and usually were made of oak. The wood was left natural so that the graining and organic nature of the material would clearly show. The simplicity of the freestanding pieces made the design suitable for machine manufacturing, although Wright did not design a line of commercial furniture until the 1950s when he was in his late eighties.

One way Prairie School architects blended architecture and design was by using built-in furniture. This was not a new innovation in furniture design as the Shakers had also specialized in building cabinetry into walls. However, Wright and other notable Prairie School architects such as George Washington Maher and George Grant Elmslie took the concept of built-ins a step further and used them as part of the interior architecture of a house. For example, cabinetry would often be placed to design a specific activity area within a larger room. Thus, while blocking the view, they did not interrupt the free flow of space, which is essential in an open-plan arrangement.

Elmslie and Purcell also designed this striking mahogany clock with brass inlay in 1912 for the Henry B. Babson House by Louis Sullivan in Riverside, Illinois.

FOLK TRADITION

Brightly colored chintzes are incorporated into this nineteenth-century "Lone Star" quilt.

The pioneers who settled the ever-expanding frontier were a hardy and resourceful group. It often goes unrecognized that they were also creative and artful. Their creativity showed through in their ability to make what they needed to farm the land and to build shelter, and many of their handicrafts are quite beautiful.

Frontier women, in particular, were resourceful in making comfortable homes with little in the way of outside help or goods. The techniques of various handicrafts, but particularly needlework, were passed down from mother to daughter.

Frontier women were expected to provide the nicest home environment possible, and their handicrafts display a high degree of creativity. Lacking almost all the conveniences—including shops and decorating magazines—to disseminate style and supply instructions for making household and decorative items, these women excelled at making colorful patchwork quilts from tiny bits of leftover fabric. Patterns generally were square, although rare quilts have patterns in the shapes of hexagons or triangles. The landscape was a popular decorative motif. Some motifs were structural, showing the log cabin and the school house, while others were naturalistic, showing flowers, the sun, and the stars.

CHAPTER

THIRTEEN ■

The West is the land of eclecticism. Settled for the most part after the introduction of mass-produced furniture in the 1840s, the houses of the West reflect a marriage between the national mass market and the uniquely regional, both old and new.

"From the brutalist to the funky, from the eclectic to the minimal—California has it all," noted Susan S. Szenasy of *Residential Interiors* magazine in 1979. "It is a region with a definite identity, established by individuals with a sense of self-worth and understanding of their unique environment. As we struggle to break through the homogenizing film that covers our mass-cultured land, we need to take another look at California and learn."

In many ways, the West—California, in particular—leads the way in interior design. Concepts developed there are adopted —and adapted—by designers throughout the country. In recent years, California designers have led the way in developing exterior living areas and integrating the indoor and outdoor environments. Almost single-handedly, they have spread the new design gospel that calls for informal rooms; sparked a renaissance in the use of natural materials and varied fabric textures; and championed contemporary crafts while revolutionizing the way we look at and use color.

Not surprisingly, California designers led the nation in bringing the outdoors inside. In this instance, glazing brightens a soaring, two-story living space.

WESTERN ECLECTICISM

Simple open shelving and rustic furnishings are deftly woven into a contemporary kitchen plan.

Nowhere in the country is interior design as varied as in the West. Firmly entrenched in tradition, eclecticism arose in the nineteenth century from the need to transport furnishings from the East. Western interiors always have possessed a riotous mix of the imported (even if only from the Midwest) and the homegrown.

The practice is vividly illustrated in as diverse places as California and Idaho, where early twentieth-century log cabin rooms are enlivened by the new-fangled phonograph of turn-of-the-century technology or the delicacy of an Art Nouveau vase. Westerners proudly carry on the exciting spirit of eclecticism today. A new house, for example, may offer the silhouette of a solar house on the exterior. Indoors, however, the visitor is apt to find hand-crafted glasswork inspired by the Art Nouveau style; thick, slab-like, hand-carved wood tables, and plush velvet upholstery saturated with colors straight from Victorian America.

While part of the reason for eclecticism is rooted in the quest for individual expression, in the West it is also practical. The extensive use of glazing to bring sun and views indoors creates bright and airy interiors that cry out for the visually softening effect of wood cabinetry and furniture with soft upholstery.

THE ARTS AND CRAFTS TRADITION

Horizontal lines mark the furnishings in the Gamble house in Pasadena.

Most people would associate the Arts and Crafts Movement with California. Indeed, the Mission-Style furniture label that grew out of this movement is named—and, in some cases, patterned—after the furnishings of the Franciscan missions of California. Most Mission-Style furniture was manufactured elsewhere, primarily in the Midwest and the East (see pages 192–94). However, these pieces have found the perfect home in the interiors of the West. The tradition of using Arts and Crafts pieces in Western rooms goes back to the beginning of the movement when they blended well with walls composed of logs.

The preeminent devotees of this movement on the West Coast were the Greene brothers—Charles S. and Henry M. To these architects, the furnishings for a house were as important as the architecture. Their work reflects the influences of a number of international design themes—Japanese, Scandinavian, and Tibetan—interwoven into houses uniquely suited to the climatic conditions and building sites of California (see pages 120–21).

Some of these are evident in the Gamble House in Pasadena where both the architecture and the interior design is governed by the horizontal planes associated with the Japanese aesthetic. Like adherents of the Prairie School, the Greene brothers designed built-in cabinetry that blended into the architecture so that the two elements—often at clashing odds— became one. This approach was part of the brothers' goal in designing and building houses: to create an environment that was simple and direct in its function while being beautiful in its appearance.

Mission-Style furniture is enjoying unprecedented popularity all across the country today. But no where does it mesh with architecture and design than in the sundrenched rooms of California. Because of the popularity of Mission-Style furniture, some notable pieces are being manufactured for the contemporary home furnishings market. Some are reproductions of pieces that originated in California. Others are adaptations of original designs and generally bear labels reading "inspired by."

Sculptural lines and exquisite detailing mark this Arts and Crafts rocker.

Graceful curves flare gently outward to the bottom of this lovely silver service dating from the Arts and Crafts era. The finely crafted service is part of—and displayed in—the Gamble house in Pasadena, California, which has been designated a national historic landmark.

Arts and Crafts furnishings look right at home in a California bungalow.

RANCH FURNITURE

Firmly set in the rustic tradition, ranch furniture represents the Western pioneers' solutions to accommodate the universal needs for eating, sleeping, and seating. It is the type of furniture that is most associated with the West. Like Mission-Style furniture, ranch pieces are simple and straightforward. Constructed of hard woods, they are extremely durable and have served some families for many generations. The favored upholstery material is leather, which often is used in bright primary colors such as red.

Juxtaposed with the furniture are textiles that are made or inspired by the designs of Native Americans.

Because they defy stylistic categorization and are often crude in their execution, ranch furnishings are not recognized as high decorative art. However, in their natural habitat, ranch furnishings do look artful. As a result, many examples of ranch furnishings have fallen into the category of "country" and are widely sought after by decorators and their clients who favor that style.

In a new house in Santa Fe, old traditions thrive, from the beamed ceilings to the sculpted fireplace and the thick timbers supporting the roof.

The thick white walls of the New Mexico adobe house contrast with wood ceilings and supply plenty of space for deep, built-in bookcases.

DETAILS AND FLOURISHES

PART IV

CHAPTER
FOURTEEN ■

Details give architecture much of its charm and individuality. Sometimes they are used to create a focal point which the viewer's eye hooks onto and thus, serve as an anchor for visually experiencing the entire structure. They unite the interior design with the exterior architecture and extend the structure, if only symbolically, to the outdoors so that it blends with its site.

Every regional architectural style in America embodies its own unique method of detailing, whether it is the design of the roof overhang, porch, doorway, fence, or columns. As homeowners return and see the familiar form of their house and its distinctive architectural details, they know that they are home. For the visitor, details enliven the architecture and, just as importantly, set the tone for what is to come.

Americans have always realized the importance of detailing. As a result, when they built houses, they included designs for architectural embellishment. Even the flat, unadorned walls of the sparest colonial houses are often punctuated with the unexpected visual stimulus of an elaborately carved front door. Besides creating the necessary point of focus for the entire house, the doorway beckons visitors toward the entry and raises the simple act of arriving—or returning home—to a ceremonial level.

This dome in New Mexico reflects the Moorish influences on the architecture of the Southwest.

THE NORTHEAST

In Deerfield, Mass., an elaborate colonial door has been preserved.

Woody Schempp reproduced a similar door for a new house.

Because their houses were so plain and unadorned, colonial Americans took great pains to create an aura of elegance with exterior details. The front door of the square frame Saltbox house, for example, is often adorned with decoration inspired by classical or Rococo design, which colonial craftsmen carved with exquisite attention to detail.

A number of colonial entryways are preserved in the historic houses of Deerfield, Massachusetts. There, they form a living his-

tory of architecture and inspire new interpretations and reproductions. A case in point is a door on a Deerfield house that contemporary woodworker Woody Schempp painstakingly reproduced for a new house.

In some cases, local tradition dictated that the front door be left plain and undecorated. In that case, the emphasis on detailing shifted to the first-floor windows, which often were embellished with classically inspired pediments. Later, when front porches became popular, the ceiling of the protective overhang was often detailed with timber beams.

On the roof, cupolas were given a finishing—and functional—crown in the form of a weathervane. These handwrought examples of metalwork add distinction much like the spire on skyscrapers built in the twentieth century.

Fences and other outdoor dividers of property and space made for much more than good neighbors in the Northeast. They also became works of art in their own right. Some show a careful attention to detail with rails of staggered heights that create an undulating line that "leads" the eye across the length and width of the property. Others, built at a uniform height march straightforwardly across the enclosure but are enlivened by small heart-shaped carvings at the top. Regardless of the approach taken, almost all had ornamented corner posts with carefully carved tops that inject a note of contrast with the rest of the fence and clearly define the landscape.

Latticework has proven a practical outdoor screening strategy that serves as a windbreak in winter while softening sunlight in summer. In addition, the latticework shields backyards from street view and acts as a trellis for growing vines.

Latticework is a familiar motif in many parts of the Northeast.

The picket fence is an historic method of defining property boundaries in small New England hamlets.

THE SOUTH

Classically inspired columns mark the entries of many Charleston town houses.

Architectural details in the South range from the classicial elegance of the high styles found in older cities to the plain and austere finishes of rural areas. With its many old town houses, the city of Charleston, South Carolina, is a treasure trove of classical elements. The exterior doorways of the Charleston Single open directly onto the street and bespeak a time when visiting friends and neighbors was an important social occasion. To reinforce this idea, the exterior doorways are flanked by support columns and topped with windows, pediments, and sometimes both.

To offset the massing of columns and other decorative motifs, entries were fitted with an abundance of glazing. Usually this was an arrangement of small panes, sometimes in complicated patterns. In other instances, the glazing was arranged as bands of beveled-edge glass around doorways.

The classical columns at the entry of this Southern mansion are offset by the lightness of a band of beveled glass positioned above the open doorway.

A sweeping porch embellishes the corner of a Charleston town house.

Porches, balconies, and verandas took on special significance in the South for their ability to shelter open windows and doorways, thus encouraging cross-ventilation even during rainstorms. Tucked on the side away from the street-facing elevation, these outdoor areas increased living space during the long warm season and sheltered rooms from direct sunlight. Generally, they carried through the decorative carving utilized throughout the exterior including the use of handrailings and columns for structural support on both the first and second floors. The incorporation of columns into the structure extended from the cities to rural areas

A Southern house porch extends the width of the structure, increasing living space.

where many plantation front porches were defined by simpler interpretations of this classical element.

The cupola, a mainstay of the Southern architecture, has been updated by architect Robert Ford, who teaches at Mississippi State University. His cupola is designed in a flat, contemporary mode. Still, its glazed panels at the top open to allow hot air to escape. Though new, the house abounds in historical Southern motifs including the clapboard siding and metal roof, which is punctuated with modern skylights. These illuminate the entry and enable direct sunlight to strike an interior Trombe wall that

Robert Ford has reinterpreted the belvedere for his solar-heated and cooled house in Mississippi.

absorbs heat and stores it until nighttime. In the Southern tradition, the entry is sheltered from harsh sun by a substantial overhang. This enabled the architect to specify an abundance of glazing at the entry so that light—but not heat—can enter the interior.

Though set at the other extreme of sophistication, log cabins built in the South had their deft touches of detailing, also. The Moravian log cabins constructed in Missouri and other locations were made of logs that were hand-hewn by local craftsmen. The ends were notched and the logs laid across each other at the corners. With this approach, they were held firmly in place by the force of gravity.

In the South, Moravian settlers built their cabins with logs that were hand-notched by local craftsmen.

THE SOUTHWEST

A Victorian house in Galveston, Texas is elevated to protect against flood tides.

Like their counterparts in the Deep South, Southwesterners have become adept at cooling their houses. One of the devices favored in the nineteenth century was the addition of a sprawling front porch. Older houses in Houston, Texas make the most of this element by extending it two stories high. The lower level is shaded by the second, which is extended high enough off the ground to catch the breeze.

The same strategy was followed by the builders of the nineteenth-century Victorian houses in nearby Galveston. Early builders took this opportunity to create small works of art by designing lovely exterior stairways that are shaped to open outward as if the house were beckoning guests to come inside. The windows

Wood framing and planks set into the adobe wall provide security for an old New Mexico house.

are guarded from wind damage by louvered storm windows, many of which are frequently embellished with ornamental motifs.

In the twentieth century, many additions to older houses have utilized the greater abundance and affordability of glass to make small spaces seem larger, create sunny indoor environments, and enhance the exterior decoration of the windows.

To shade outdoor living areas such as patios from the heat of the sun, many Southwestern houses are enlivened with imaginatively designed coverings. In Houston, that frequently results in the application of overhead latticework, which creates the atmosphere of a peaceful arbor. Besides shielding the space from the sun and allowing it to be used even in the heat of the day,

Though rarely found in the architecture of New Mexico, the arch reflects the impact of Moorish motifs on Hispanic settlers.

A cutout illustrates the thickness of old exterior adobe walls.

Rustic seating echoes the plain yet eerily beautiful adobe wall and window opening of a New Mexico house.

the latticework creates a cool setting where plants can flourish.

Shading is equally important for the houses of New Mexico but it is accomplished with a distinctly regional twist. In that arid region, patios are often protected with an extension of the main roof. Beyond that extend *vigas* made of timbers, an historic decorative motif. Latticework is utilized to shade porches and walkways. However, instead of the dainty white latticework a visitor might find in New England or in the Deep South, here the sunlight is diffused with criss-crossing designs made of logs.

The doorways of New Mexico come in an infinite variety. Those guarding the privacy of great old estates are massive constructions of wood, squat ornamental columns, and huge walls. Others protecting the security and privacy of more humble houses

often consist only of planking set in an adobe or wood frame.

The walls defining property are often spiced with exterior openings revealing their thickness. Those that merely define outlying boundaries of specific areas within a compound are generally left open. Others, especially those that open directly onto the street, can be closed off with shutters in simple designs. The windows in many houses, on the other hand, often appear as if they were simply cut into the walls as needed.

The architecture of New Mexico has been influenced strongly by international design. Though rare, the dome reflects the Spanish adoption of many Moorish motifs. The dome and its close counterpart, the arch, have been translated by New Mexico craftsmen into varied doorways and passageways.

THE MIDWEST

Colored bands of stonework emphasize the lateral lines of the Glessner House and visually relieve its massing of architectural elements.

Stone fashioned into rectangular blocks and fans distinguishes the Glessner House.

Architectural detailing in this part of the country is often associated with the Prairie School as exemplified in the work of Frank Lloyd Wright. However, some of the most beautiful examples of exterior detailing in the Midwest can be seen in the work of Henry Hobson Richardson. His Glessner House is immediately identifiable by its distinctive stonework, which has been cut and assembled to create a visually heavy appearance that evokes the image of layers of ancient geological strata. The fan motif seen executed in glass above the front doors of many Charleston, South Carolina, town houses is repeated in the Midwest but in stone. While the motif may be the same, its rendering in a different material imbues the architecture with an entirely new sense. In Charleston, the motif lightens the ornate carving of the entryway and brightens the interior. By contrast, in the Glessner House, it adds to the sense of weightiness and in the mind's eye recalls the Norman houses of France, which served as the model for the design.

The long, low architecture of the house is reinforced by bands of contrasting colored stone that emphasize the horizontal lines of the house. Vertical elements—chimneys and roofs varying in shape from the conical to the steeply pitched gable—draw the viewer's eye upward lessening the impact of the huge house.

The massiveness of the stonework is lightened considerably by lacy, delicate metalwork blending artful decorative scrolls with a note of practicality—the street address.

THE WEST

Decorative glass and woodwork—much machine-made—embellish a Victorian house in San Francisco.

The fanciful woodwork of many of San Francisco's Victorian houses has been highlighted with intriguing colors.

Because Westerners always have been intimately linked to the land, architects in this region of the country frequently draw upon nature for the materials and colors of their exterior detailing. Historically, stone and sod were utilized as primitive building materials in North Dakota to create entire houses as well as construction elements including foundations and exterior walls. Stones of varying shapes and sizes were carefully layered enhancing stability and resulting in great visual appeal when studied closely. For even more protection against disintegration, early builders constructed their walls with generous portion of sod, often mixed with grasses, set between the layers of stone.

Detailing in the nineteenth century was by no means limited to the hand-hewn. The development of mechanical saws enabled builders to add whatever trim and details they desired. Some of this is quite elegant; on other houses, the detailing seems excessive and reveals the Victorians' struggle to come to terms with

the machine age. On many Victorian houses, bay windows are emphasized with decorative woodwork in geometric, often diamond-shaped, designs. Many of these have been highlighted by the application of varying shades of the same color on one house to starkly contrasting colors on another. A quick trip through the color spectrum with only a few inches of wood separating light and dark tones distinguishes other houses. When blended with an abundance of machine carving, the overall effect is fanciful or ludicrous, depending on the viewer's individual aesthetic.

Of course, detailing is at its best when it is restrained. Many Western houses reflect this subdued approach by embodying classically inspired carving applied to support columns. Decorative embellments, however, need not be restricted to wood. A front door becomes an enticing and attractive focal point for the facade of a house when the center section is filled with a large piece of beautifully etched glass.

Today, the reliance on nature continues. A new house in the desert echoes the colors of the landscape while providing luxurious contemporary shelter. At the entry to the property, stylized ornamental gates define the compound. Visitors walk through arches, an historic motif that has been restated here in the form of contemporary geometric shapes set within a gentle curve.

Inside, the emphasis on architectural geometry continues. Sleekly curved walls, flights of exterior stairs, and dividing walls are all imbued with a sculptural air and painted with the beiges and whites of the desert. To break up the strict lines and hard planes, the architects added a bit of modern whimsy—an undulating curved wall at the end of a covered passageway.

Shaded walkways to shield the house from the intense sunlight abound in the compound. Many are curvelike and protected by a thick roof. Periodic support pillars are detailed in contrasing white to evoke the highly stylized image of an ancient design element—the column.

The gentle curves of these stylized gates harmonize with the graceful lines of the house design and the rolling natural landscape it is set in.

CHAPTER

FIFTEEN ■

While the exterior of a house makes a statement about the owners to the public, the interior tells a far different story. It is indoors where the owners reveal themselves to themselves, where they transform empty spaces into comfortable rooms by imbuing them with a feeling of place. Details humanize a structure by giving us the reassurance of familiar forms that enable us to feel comfortable even when we are in unfamiliar surroundings.

Interior detailing varies considerably across the country. But some elements remain intact—indigenous materials, native forms and decorative motifs, and colors drawn from the natural surroundings. Some are historically inspired, others are new and representative of our own time. Yet all work together to create a sense of dwelling.

The darkly stained woodwork and trim in the Manship House that so perfectly evokes the feeling of the Victorian era is offset by period-style decorating that includes ruby-red draperies and colorful patterned carpets.

THE NORTHEAST

In the houses of this region, fine craftsmanship is a hallowed tradition dating back to the early settlers. Houses built in the colonial era may have been sparsely furnished, but the walls would often be awash with decorative, intricately carved woodwork. Besides adding to the overall beauty of the structure, the woodwork also served as an added layer of insulation against the winter cold.

Fine examples of the woodworking crafts can be found in the stairways of humble eighteenth-century houses as well as along the walls and doors of nineteenth-century high-style town houses of New York City. In tandem with the woodwork is an emphasis on small but practical embellishments including hardware, which was usually handforged.

Among the favorite decorative techniques in the Northeast was the art of stenciling in a wide variety of designs. This old craft form has been revived recently as designers and home owners attempt to inject a feeling of place into sterile-looking new houses. As a result, old designs, particularly borders, have been utilized as decorative frames for contemporary window walls in new houses. The popularity of stenciled borders has prompted manufacturers of wallpapers and other wallcovering products to offer an assortment of decorative borders that imitate stenciling.

In a New York City town house, long-neglected albeit fine woodwork has been expertly restored to its original glory by Bader Binter, Inc. The thick wood protects the owners from winter cold and neighbors' noise.

An eighteenth-century hand-forged door latch graces a 1720 door in a New England historic house. Small touches such as the elongated shape give this everyday item a great sense of elegance and old-time charm.

A stenciled floral pattern by artist Leslie Powers is imbued with the Victorian spirit in its extreme amount of shading and detailing in both the flowers and leaves as well as in its subdued choice of colors.

THE SOUTH

Formal house styles in the South historically have been marked by their abundance of classical, European-derived detailing. The care given to finishing the interiors of these houses is particularly evident in the woodwork, which is often elegant and intricately carved. For example, ornately carved paneling graced houses in the cities and many rural plantations of the wealthy landed gentry.

An emphasis on wood trim is prevalent in the baseboards and crown moldings. A favored wall treatment in both the eighteenth and nineteenth centuries in the South was wainscoting. Generally, the wainscoting was painted a contrasting color—usually darker—to the upper portion of the wall. In simpler houses, wainscoting might be eliminated in favor of streamlined chair or plate rails. A chair rail is a thick strip of decorative molding that runs laterally across the face of the wall. It is set approximately at the height of a chair from the floor and protects the wall from damage when chairs are moved in and out from the dining table. A plate rail is set higher and stands out farther from the wall surface. It was utilized as a display space for decorative plates set on pedestal display racks.

Other wood embellishments were part and parcel of the interior architecture. One of the most common of these in houses of the wealthy was the bowfat, a buffet built into the dining room wall. These pieces were decorated with displays of fine dinnerware collected by the family. Doors became a decorative element, too, when they were graced with carved panels in bold geometric designs. Often they were imbued with a straited effect created from the handsaws and other finishing tools that were the trade of the woodcarver.

The abundance of woodwork in Southern houses is often visually offset by huge concentrations of masonry. Large brick fireplaces for cooking and heating fill the walls of many rooms in elegant urban houses as well as in rural estates. Outbuildings on country property also had individual fireplaces that were less elaborate and sometimes used for working. Depending on the degree of embellishment, fireplaces might be left with simple, unadorned firebox openings or fitted with marble mantels topped with wood carved to resemble the capitals of classical columns.

Dark woodwork and heavily patterned wallpaper reflects Victorian Gothic Revival influences in a bedroom of the Manship House.

THE SOUTHWEST

The dining room of a contemporary adobe house is defined by a sculptural curving partial wall.

The colors of the earth set the tone for Southwestern interiors. But instead of the bland beige-after-beige series of rooms one might expect, Southwesterners weave the earth tones into a soothing backdrop for bright furnishings and accessories.

In New Mexico, white or beige walls are *de rigeur* for old and new adobe construction. They complement the dark brick floors that add a natural note and visual texture. Spicing up this basic foundation for decorating are generous applications of wood.

One of the most frequently encountered applications of wood in the Southwest is not for floors or paneling—but for ceilings. Here, alternating patterns of planking create an arresting pattern that draws the eye to the upper portion of the room. To support the wood ceiling, large timbers that have been stripped of their bark are set in evenly spaced rows. Breaking up the continuity of the ceiling treatment are skylights—sometimes operable, sometimes not—that flood the interior with natural light.

Ornamental woodwork extends to windows and doors. In this context, they draw attention to the passageways into other rooms while serving as support frames. Usually, the wood is left in its natural state—or it is stained to preserve that look. One of the favored woods in the Southwest is the native Ponderosa pine, which has a light and beautiful yellow cast in its natural state. This ancient material has been crafted into many contemporary modes including sleeping lofts and large-scale cabinetry.

In traditional adobe construction, almost every room has a fireplace. Though this is a constant, the shapes they assume are not. Some are handsculpted into horseshoe shapes while others are oval, square, and rectangular.

The kitchen echoes the surface treatments in the living room while providing modern conveniences and appliances.

In a contemporary house, traditional *vigas* and *latillas* tower over stucco walls and brick floors.

THE MIDWEST

Beautiful woodwork draws the eye upward emphasizing the airy volumes of Prairie School houses.

Wood is the favored material for adding zest and architectural interest in the houses of the Midwest. Frequently, the walls of early twentieth-century houses were entirely paneled creating a stately environment for the furnishings of the Arts and Crafts Movement that flourished in the Midwest around Chicago. The paneling also served as a subtle, monochromatic backdrop for furniture, upholstery, which tended to be heavily tufted.

Instead of full paneling, rooms in the Midwest sometimes were ringed with crown molding. While the area below this ornamental woodwork was finished with plaster, the area above, including the ceiling, was highlighted by the application of wallpaper with large-scale designs.

Wood detailing figures heavily in the work of the Prairie School of architects. In houses designed by Frank Lloyd Wright, ornamental woodwork relected the design of the furnishings, which created a unified, all-of-a-piece interior. For example, stair bannisters, consisting of thin strips of wood set vertically, echoed the design of many chair backs. For contrast, decorative molding was arranged in bands and placed near the tops of walls to draw attention to the upper portion of the room.

While the walls in these rooms were merely framed in wood, stairwells and other connecting spaces were set apart visually by an application of wainscoting. This indicated a change in the purpose of the space and protected the walls in highly traveled—but narrow—spaces from damage from scraping and banging.

Wood also was applied to ceilings in the form of beamwork. Like other woodwork, beams were left their natural color to contrast with other, light-hued surfaces and to add a note of warmth.

In the same house, the wood paneling rises up the stairwell protecting the plaster walls from damage.

Extensive paneling follows the curve of the wall in the foyer of a Prairie School house. The curve is visually emphasized by molding.

THE WEST

The tradition of eclecticism on the West Coast oftens leads to visually intriguing and fanciful combinations of exterior and interior detailing. The Bay Area Style that is indigenous to San Francisco is a case in point. In a house designed by Stephen Lubin, the interior is marked by soaring spaces, large windows, stucco walls, and furnishings that bespeak the California lifestyle— wicker, weavings, and light-colored fabrics. One of the unusual and endearing characteristics of the Bay Area Style is its reinterpretation of classical elements. For example, the large-scale, curve-topped Palladian window is rendered in an unusual, highly stylized form in an unlikely place—the kitchen. But this window is no mere decorative grandstand. Instead, it commands a lovely outdoor view and brightens the breakfast area. Though an unabashedly modern version of the Bay Area Style, this house embodies an extensive use of local building products creating a warm and welcoming atmosphere. In keeping with the informality inherent in the Bay Area Style, shelving is open easing access to the essentials of cooking oriented collectibles.

The bungalows of Greene & Greene are a showcase for the fine, handcrafted detailing of the Arts and Crafts Movement in California. The interior of the Gamble House in Pasadena is custom-designed throughout—from the furniture, built-in cabinetry and paneling to the rugs, lighting, stained glass and accessories. Teak, maple, Port Orford cedar, redwood, and oak were selected for the interior finishes and furniture. Each piece of furniture was hand-rubbed to a satiny finish. Doors, windows, and light fixtures are embellished with iridescent Tiffany glass.

In rural areas, detailing was much less elegant but still interesting and, most of all, appropriate. Even today, country houses in the West incorporate the age-old materials of this region including an abundance of brick and redwood. When James Slenes of BJSS Architects in Olympia, Washington, designed a new house, he included a farmhouse style, shed-roof extension that contains the large kitchen. Reminiscent of the expansive kitchens of nineteenth-century farmsteads, this one includes space for working and informal dining. Though narrow, it seems much larger because of the sloping ceiling and skylights. The height of the space is accentuated by a brick wall and crossbeams. Ceiling fans and cabinetry help recall the stylistic origins of the contemporary Western farmhouse.

In the Gamble House, all interior paneling, cabinetry and furniture was custom designed.

Architectural Record, all issues, 1980–1986.

Brolin, Brent C. *Architecture in Context—Fitting New Buildings with Old*. New York: Van Nostrand Reinhold Co., 1980.

Brunt, Andrew. *Phaidon Guide to Furniture*. Englewood Cliffs, N.J.: Prentice-Hall, Inc., 1983.

Bunting, Bainbridge. *John Gaw Meem—Southwestern Architect*. Albuquerque, N.M.: University of New Mexico Press, 1983.

Cathers, David M. *Furniture of the American Arts and Crafts Movement*. New York: The New American Library, Inc., 1981.

Comstock, Helen. *American Furniture*. New York: The Viking Press Inc., 1962.

Darling, Sharon. *Chicago Furniture: Art, Craft, & Industry, 1833–1983*. New York: W. W. Norton & Co., in association with The Chicago Historical Society, 1984.

Emmerling, Mary. *Mary Emmerling's American Country West*. New York: Clarkson N. Potter, Inc., 1985.

Fitch, James Marston. *American Building 2: The Environmental Forces that Shape It*. New York: Schocken Books, 1975.

Foley, Mary Mix. *The American House*. New York: Harper & Row, 1980.

Gebhard, David and Deborah Nevins. *200 Years of American Architectural Drawing*. New York: Whitney Library of Design, 1977.

Harrison, Henry S. *Houses*. New York: Charles Scribner's Sons, 1973.

Home, all issues, 1980–1985.

Horn, Richard. *Fifties Style: Then and Now*. New York: Beech Tree Books, William Morrow and Company, Inc., 1985.

House Beautiful's Building Manual, all issues, 1980–1986.

Jackson, John Brinckerhoff. *Discovering the Vernacular Landscape*. New Haven, Conn.: Yale University Press, 1984.

Lancaster, Clay. *The American Bungalow, 1880–1930*. New York: Abbeville Press, Inc., 1985.

Madigan, Mary Jean, ed. *Nineteenth Century Furniture: Innovation, Revival and Reform*. New York: Billboard Publications, Inc., 1982.

Manchester, William. *The Glory and the Dream*. Boston: Little, Brown and Co., 1974.

Moholy-Nagy, Sibyl. *Native Genius in American Architecture*. New York: Horizon Press Inc., 1957.

Moore, Charles, Kathryn Smith, and Peter Becker. *Home Sweet Home: American Domestic Vernacular Architecture*. New York: Rizzoli International Publications Inc. in association with the Craft and Folk Art Museum, Los Angeles, Calif., 1983.

National Trust for Historic Preservation. *America's Forgotten Architecture*. New York: Pantheon Books, 1976.

Oates, Phyllis Bennett. *The Story of Western Furniture*. New York: Harper & Row, 1981.

Osborn, Susan. *American Rustic Furniture*. New York: Harmony Books, 1984.

Page, Marian. *Furniture Designed by Architects*. New York: Whitney Library of Design, 1980.

Progressive Architecture, all issues, 1980–1986.

Schwartz, Marvin D. *Chairs, Tables, Sofas & Beds*. New York: Alfred A. Knopf, 1982.

M: Manufacturer or distributor

MO: Mail order

R: Retail store

T: To the trade only

Send inquiries to the address listed for retail outlets in your area that sell this company's products.

ACCESSORIES

BASKETS/BOWLS

AMERICA HURRAH ANTIQUES▪R
766 MADISON AVE.▪NEW YORK, N.Y. 10021

CONNECTICUT BASKET WORKS▪R, MO
1262 MADISON AVE.▪NEW YORK, N.Y. 10028

COTTERILL & CO.▪MO
1119 S. LA BREA AVE.▪LOS ANGELES, CALIF. 90019

THE COUNTRY LOFT▪MO
S. SHORE PARK▪HINGHAM, MASS. 02043

CRAFT HOUSE▪R, MO
COLONIAL WILLIAMSBURG▪WILLIAMSBURG, VA. 23185

GORDON FOSTER ANTIQUES▪R
1322 THIRD AVE.▪NEW YORK, N.Y. 10021

LILLIAN VERNON▪MO
510 S. FULTON ST.▪MT. VERNON, N.Y. 10550

MARTHA WETHERBEE BASKETS▪R, MO
STAR RTE., BOX 35▪SANBORTON, N.H. 03269

THE YELLOW MONKEY ANTIQUES▪R
YELLOW MONKEY VILLAGE▪RTE. 35▪CROSS RIVER, N.Y. 10518

BEDSPREADS

BATES FABRICS, INC.▪M
1431 BROADWAY▪NEW YORK, N.Y. 10018

BLANKETS

NATURALLY BRITISH▪M
P. O. BOX 347▪ALEXANDRIA, VA. 22313

CANDLESTICKS

COLONIAL CANDLE GIFT SHOP▪R
MAIN ST.▪HYANNIS, MASS. 02601

CLOCKS

CHELSEA CLOCK CO.▪M
284 EVERETT AVE.▪CHELSEA, MASS. 02150

DINNERWARE

JOSIAH WEDGWOOD & SONS·M
41 MADISON AVE.·NEW YORK, N.Y. 10010

FIREPLACE ACCESSORIES

THE HARVIN CO.·M
BOX 500·WAYNESBORO, VA. 22980

LIGHTING FIXTURES

REJUVENATION HOUSE PARTS·M
901 N. SKIDMORE·PORTLAND, OREG. 97217

VIRGINIA METALCRAFTERS
1010 E. MAIN STREET·WAYNESBORO, VA. 22980

METALWORK

THE ESSEX FORGE·M
OLD DENNISON RD.·ESSEX, CONN. 06426

GOOD DIRECTIONS, INC.·M
24 ARDMORE RD.·STAMFORD, CONN. 06902

LUNT SILVERSMITHS·M
GREENFIELD, MASS. 01302

VIRGINIA METALCRAFTERS·M
1010 E. MAIN ST.·WAYNESBORO, VA. 22980

VASES

ARTISAN GALLERIES·R
2100 A–3 N. HASKELL·DALLAS, TEX. 75204

LINDQUIST STUDIOS GALLERY·R
PATCH RD.·HENNIKER, N.H. 03242

ANTIQUE FURNITURE

The availability of regional furnishings will vary depending on each retailer's stock supply at any given time.

DIDIER AARON·R
32 E. 67TH ST.·NEW YORK, N.Y. 10021

BOB BAHSSIN·R
POST OAK GALLERY·2128 BOSTON POST RD.·LARCHMONT, N.Y. 10538

JEAN PAUL BEAUJARD·R
209 E. 76TH ST.·NEW YORK, N.Y. 10021

JOAN BOGART ANTIQUES·R
BOX 265·ROCKVILLE CENTER, N.Y. 11571

MARGARET B. CALDWELL·R
142 E. 82ND ST.·NEW YORK, N.Y. 10028

E.J. CANTON·R
818 MORRIS AVE.·LUTHERVILLE, MD. 21093

THE CHATELAINE SHOP·R
BOX 436·GEORGETOWN, CONN. 06829

RICHARD AND EILEEN DUBROW·R
BOX 128·BAYSIDE, N.Y. 11361

MIMI FINDLAY ANTIQUES·R
1556 THIRD AVE.·NEW YORK, N.Y. 10028

HAMILTON–HYRE·R
413 BLEECKER ST.·NEW YORK, N.Y. 10014

PETER HILL, INC.·R
MAPLEWOOD MANOR·EAST LEMPSTER, N.H. 03605

MARGOT JOHNSON, INC.·R
40 W. 40TH ST.·NEW YORK, N.Y. 10018

JORDAN–VOLPE GALLERY·R
457 W. BROADWAY·NEW YORK, N.Y. 10012

KATHY KURLAND·R
1435 LEXINGTON AVE.·NEW YORK, N.Y. 10028

H.M. LUTHER, INC.▪R
61 E. 11TH ST.▪NEW YORK, N.Y. 10003

RICHARD McGEEHAN▪R
BOX 181▪BEDFORD HILLS, N.Y. 10507

DON MAGNER▪R
309 HENRY ST.▪BROOKLYN, N.Y. 11201

FLORIAN PAPP, INC.▪R
962 MADISON AVE.▪NEW YORK, N.Y. 10021

ARCHITECTS AND BUILDERS

BADER BINTER
39 PROSPECT PLACE▪BROOKLYN, N.Y. 10118

BENSON WOODWORKING
BOX 224, RR 1▪ALSTEAD, N.H. 03602

ROBERT S. BENNETT
65 S. MAIN ST.▪PENNINGTON, N.J. 08534

BLUE/SUN LTD.
P.O. BOX 118▪FARMINGTON, CONN. 06032

TURNER BROOKS
BOX 139, RD 1▪STARKSBORO, VT. 05487

TERRY BROWN
2661 HARRISON AVE.▪CINCINNATI, OHIO 45211

CENTERBROOK (formerly MOORE GROVER HARPER)
67 MAIN ST.▪CENTERBROOK, CONN. 06426

THE 18TH CENTURY COMPANY
▪BILL AND MARILYN NORTON
WOODLAND DR.▪DURHAM, CONN. 06422

ROBERT FORD
BOX 1438▪MISSISSIPPI STATE, MISS. 39762

GRATTAN GILL
128 ROUTE 6A▪SANDWICH, MASS. 02563

GRAHAM GUND ASSOCIATES
12 ARROW ST.▪CAMBRIDGE, MASS. 02138

DON M. HISAKA & ASSOCIATES
1000 MASSACHUSETTS AVE.▪CAMBRIDGE, MASS. 02138

JSA INC.
439 MIDDLE ST.▪PORTSMOUTH, N.H. 03801

HUGH NEWELL JACOBSEN
2529 P ST. N.W.▪WASHINGTON, D.C. 20007

KELBAUGH & LEE ARCHITECTS
240 NASSAU ST.▪PRINCETON, N.J. 08540

WILLIAM LIPSEY
BOX 3203▪ASPEN, COLO. 81611

ORR & TAYLOR
688 ORANGE ST.▪NEW HAVEN, CONN. 06511

PAGE, ANDERSON & TURNBULL, INC.
364 BUSH ST.▪SAN FRANCISCO, CALIF. 94104

THOMPSON E. PENNEY
24 N. MARKET ST., SUITE 300▪CHARLESTON, S.C. 29401

LYMAN S.A. PERRY
311 N. NEWTOWN ST. RD.▪NEWTOWN SQUARE, PA. 19073

WARREN PLATNER (via BOB PERRON)
18 MITCHELL DR.▪NEW HAVEN, CONN. 06511

WILLIAM RAWN ASSOCIATES
101 TREMONT ST., SUITE 201▪BOSTON, MASS. 02108

BILL RIESBERG
25 ARABIAN DR.▪CHARLESTON, S.C. 29407

ROBERT A.M. STERN
211 W. 61 ST.▪NEW YORK, N.Y. 10023

RICHARD SWIBOLD
COLLINSVILLE, CONN. 06022

TAFT ARCHITECTS
807 PEDEN ST.▪HOUSTON, TEX. 77006

UKZ
190 PLEASANT GROVE RD.
G4▪ITHACA, N.Y. 14850

VENTURI, RAUCH AND SCOTT BROWN
4236 MAIN ST.▪PHILADELPHIA, PA. 19127

RIC WEINSCHENK
19 SOUTH ST.▪PORTLAND, MAINE

WILLIS & ASSOCIATES
545 MISSION ST.▪SAN FRANCISCO, CALIF. 94105

PETER WOERNER
THE BOATHOUSE▪74 FORBES AVE.▪NEW HAVEN, CONN. 06512

AUCTION HOUSES

CHRISTIE'S▪R
502 PARK AVE.▪NEW YORK, N.Y. 10022

SOTHEBY'S▪R
1334 YORK AVE.▪NEW YORK, N.Y. 10021

CRAFT GALLERIES

JACKIE CHALKLEY▪R
3301 NEW MEXICO AVE.▪WASHINGTON, D.C. 20016

COMPOSITION▪R
2801 LEAVENWORTH▪SAN FRANCISCO, CALIF. 94133

CRAFT AND FOLK ART MUSEUM▪R
5817 WILSHIRE BLVD.▪LOS ANGELES, CALIF. 90036

ELIZABETH FORTNER▪R
1114 STATE ST.▪SANTA BARBARA, CALIF. 93101

GALLERY EIGHT▪R
7464 GIRARD AVE.▪LA JOLLA, CALIF. 92037

MUSEUM OF AMERICAN FOLK ART SHOP▪R
62 W. 50TH ST.▪NEW YORK, N.Y. 10112

TEN ARROW▪R
10 ARROW ST.▪CAMBRIDGE, MASS. 02138

FLATWARE

GORHAM▪M
333 ADELAIDE AVE.▪PROVIDENCE, R.I. 02907

KIRK STIEFF CO.▪M
800 WYMAN PARK DR.▪BALTIMORE, MD. 21211

LUNT SILVERSMITHS▪M
GREENFIELD, MASS. 01302

ONEIDA SILVERSMITHS LTD.▪M
ONEIDA, N.Y. 13421

REED AND BARTON▪M
TAUNTON, MASS. 02780

TOWLE MANUFACTURING CO.▪M
114 ADDISON ST.▪BOSTON, MASS. 02128

WALLACE-INTERNATIONAL SILVERSMITHS, INC.▪M
15 STERLING DR.▪WALLINGFORD, CONN. 06492

RENOVATOR'S SUPPLY HOUSE▪M, MO
182 NORTHFIELD RD.▪MILLERS FALLS, MASS. 01349

HARDWARE

ANTIQUE HARDWARE CO.▪M
BOX 1592▪TORRANCE, CALIF. 90505

ARTISTIC BRASS▪M
3136 E. 11TH ST.▪LOS ANGELES, CALIF. 90280

CHICAGO FAUCETS▪M
2100 S. NUCLEAR DR.▪DES PLAINES, ILL. 60018

CIRECAST INC.▪M
380 7TH ST.▪SAN FRANCISCO, CALIF. 94103

CRAWFORD'S OLD HOUSE STORE▪R
301 McCALL ST.▪WAUKESHA, WIS. 53186

P.E. GUERIN▪R
23 JANE ST.▪NEW YORK, N.Y. 10014

HORTON BRASSES▪M
BOX 120▪CROMWELL, CONN. 06416

KRAFT HARDWARE▪T
300 E. 64TH ST.▪NEW YORK, N.Y. 10021

BRIAN F. LEO▪M
7520 STEVENS AVE. S.▪RICHFIELD, MINN. 55423

LITCHFIELD HOUSE▪R
CHURCH ST.▪ROXBURY, CONN. 06783

PAUL ASSOCIATES▪M
155 E. 55TH ST.▪NEW YORK, N.Y. 10022

LOCKS

FOLGER ADAM CO.▪M
P.O. BOX 688▪JOLIET, ILL. 60434

MANUFACTURED HOUSES

ACORN STRUCTURES▪M
P.O. BOX 250▪CONCORD, MASS. 01742

AMERICAN BARN CORP.▪M
(HABITAT)▪123 ELM ST.▪S. DEERFIELD, MASS. 01373

APPALACHIAN LOG STRUCTURES▪M
P.O. BOX 86▪GOSHEN, VA. 24439

AUTHENTIC HOMES▪M
P.O. BOX 1288▪LARAMIE, WYO. 82070

CEDARDALE▪M
P.O. BOX 18606▪GREENSBORO, N.C. 27419

COUNTRY LOG HOMES▪M
RTE. 7, P.O. BOX 158▪ASHLEY FALLS, MASS. 01222

DECK HOUSE▪M
930 MAIN ST.▪ACTON, MASS. 01720

GASTINEAU LOG HOMES, INC.▪M
BOX 184▪NEW BLOOMFIELD, MO. 65063

GREATWOOD LOG HOMES▪M
P.O. BOX 707▪ELKHART LAKE, WIS. 53020

GROUP III DESIGNS INC.•M
P.O. BOX 220333•CHARLOTTE, N.C. 28222

HERITAGE LOG HOMES•M
P.O. BOX 610•GATLINBURG, TENN. 37738

JUSTUS LOG HOMES•M
P.O. BOX 24426•SEATTLE, WASH. 98124

LINCOLN LOGS•M
8510 MILL RD.•CHESTERTOWN, N.Y. 12817

LINDAL CEDAR HOMES•M
P.O. BOX 24426•SEATTLE, WASH. 98124

LOK–N–LOGS•M
RD. 2, BOX 212•SHERBURNE, N.Y. 13460

LUMBER ENTERPRISES•M
75777 GALLATIN RD.•BOZEMAN, MONT. 59730

MAINE POST & BEAM CO.•M
BOX 37, RTES. 1A & 103•YORK HARBOR, MAINE 03911

MARLEY CONTINENTAL HOMES•M
7301 MISSION ROAD, SUITE 208•PRAIRIE VILLAGE, KANS. 66208

NEW ENGLAND LOG HOMES•M
2301 STATE ST.•HAMDEN, CONN. 06518

NORTHEASTERN LOG HOMES•M
P.O. BOX 126•GROTON, VT. 05046
P.O. BOX 46•KENDUSKEAG, MAINE 04450
P.O. BOX 7966•LOUISVILLE, KY. 40207

NORTHERN HOMES•M
51 GLENWOOD AVE.•GLENS FALLS, N.Y. 12801

NORTHERN PRODUCTS LOG HOMES, INC.•M
P.O. BOX 616•BANGOR, MAINE 04401

PRE–CUT INTERNATIONAL HOMES•M
P.O. BOX 886•WOODINVILLE, WASH. 98072

R&L LOG BUILDINGS•M
P.O. BOX 237•MT. UPTON, N.Y. 13809

REAL LOG HOMES•M
P.O. BOX 202•HARTLAND, VT. 05048

RIVERBEND TIMBER FRAMING, INC.•M
P.O. BOX 26•BLISSFIELD, MICH. 49228

SAWMILL RIVER POST & BEAM, INC.•M
P.O. BOX 359•LEVERETT, MASS. 01054

STONEMILL LOG HOMES•M
7015 STONEMILL RD.•KNOXVILLE, TENN. 37919

TIMBER LOG HOMES•M
AUSTIN DR. BOX 300•MARLBOROUGH, CONN. 06447

TIMBERPEG•M
P.O. BOX 1500•CLAREMONT, N.H. 03743
P.O. BOX 880•FLETCHER, N.C. 28732
P.O. BOX 8988•FT. COLLINS, COLO. 80525

TOWN & COUNTRY LOG HOMES•M
4772 U.S. 131 S.•PETOSKEY, MICH. 49770

WARD CABIN CO.•M
BOX 72•HOULTON, MAINE 04730

WESTERN LOG HOMES•M
5201 W. 48TH AVE.•DENVER, COLO. 80212

WILDERNESS LOG HOMES•M
RTE. 2–J75•PLYMOUTH, WIS. 53073

WISCONSIN LOG HOMES•M
P.O. BOX 11005•GREEN BAY, WIS. 54307

YANKEE BARN HOMES▪M
STAR RTE. B, BOX 2▪GRANTHAM, N.H. 03753

MIRRORS

FRIEDMAN BROTHERS DECORATIVE ARTS, INC.▪M
9015 N.W. 105 WAY▪MEDLEY, FLA. 33178

PAINTS

FULLER—O'BRIEN PAINTS▪M
450 E. GRAND AVE.▪SOUTH SAN FRANCISCO, CALIF. 94808

MARTIN SENOUR CO.▪M
1370 ONTARIO AVE. N.W.▪CLEVELAND, OHIO 44113

SHERWIN—WILLIAMS CO.▪M
101 PROSPECT AVE. N.W.▪CLEVELAND, OHIO 44115

POTTERY

WILLIAMSBURG POTTERY FACTORY, INC.▪M
RTE. 3, BOX 148▪LIGHTFOOT, VA. 23090

REPRODUCTION FURNITURE

AMERICAN FURNITURE GALLERIES▪M
BOX 60▪MONTGOMERY, ALA. 36101

BAKER FURNITURE CO.▪M
917 MERCHANDISE MART▪CHICAGO, ILL. 60654

COHASSET COLONIALS▪M
COHASSET, MASS. 02025

FURNITURE TRADITIONS▪M
BOX 5067▪HICKORY, N.C. 28603

GRANT'S▪M
1 WILMINGTON RD.▪LAKE PLACID, N.Y. 12946

HARDEN FURNITURE CO.▪M
MILL POND WAY▪McCONNELLSVILLE, N.Y. 13401

HICKORY CHAIR CO.▪M
P.O. BOX 2147▪HICKORY, N.C. 28603

HITCHCOCK CHAIR CO.▪M
BOX 507▪NEW HARTFORD, CONN. 06057

HOLTON FURNITURE CO.▪M
805 RANDOLPH ST.▪THOMASVILLE, N.C. 27360

MARTHA M. HOUSE▪R
1022 S. DECATUR ST.▪MONTGOMERY, ALA. 36104

KAYLYN, INC.▪M
BOX 2366▪HIGH POINT, N.C. 27261

KITTINGER CO.▪M
1893 ELMWOOD AVE.▪BUFFALO, N.Y. 14207

LANE FURNITURE CO.▪M
BOX 151▪ALTAVISTA, VA. 24517

MAGNOLIA HALL▪M
726 ANDOVER DR.▪ATLANTA, GA. 30327

RIVERSIDE FURNITURE CO.▪M
DRAWER 1427▪FORT SMITH, ARK. 72902

SHAKER WORKSHOPS▪M
P.O. BOX 1028▪CONCORD, MASS. 01742

THE STATTON FURNITURE MANUFACTURING CO.▪M
HAGERSTOWN, MD. 21740

VANGUARD FURNITURE CO.▪M
BOX 2187▪HICKORY, N.C. 28603

WEATHEREND ESTATE FURNITURE▪M
P.O. BOX 648▪ROCKPORT, MAINE 04841

WILLSBORO WOOD PRODUCTS▪M
80 BOYLSTON ST., SUITE 450▪BOSTON, MASS. 02116

TEXTILES AND WALLCOVERINGS

HERITAGE RUGS▪R
STREET RD.▪LAHASKA, PA. 18931

KARASTAN RUG MILLS▪M
919 THIRD AVE.▪NEW YORK, N.Y. 10022

KATZENBACH & WARREN, INC.▪M
950 THIRD AVE.▪NEW YORK, N.Y. 10022

LANGHORNE CARPETING CO.▪M
BOX 175▪PENNDEL, PA. 19047

MOHAWK CARPETS▪M
919 THIRD AVE.▪NEW YORK, N.Y. 10022

MONSANTO TEXTILES CO.▪M
1460 BROADWAY▪NEW YORK, N.Y. 10036

PATTERSON FLYNN & MARTIN▪T
950 THIRD AVE.▪NEW YORK, N.Y. 10022

ROSECORE CARPET CO., INC.▪M
979 THIRD AVE.▪NEW YORK, N.Y. 10022

SCALAMANDRÉ SILKS, INC.▪T
950 THIRD AVE.▪NEW YORK, N.Y. 10022

SCHUMACHER▪T
919 THIRD AVE.▪NEW YORK, N.Y. 10022

WICKER, RATTAN, AND BENT WILLOW FURNITURE

ADDED OOMPHH!▪R
270 W. WRENN ST.▪HIGH POINT, N.C. 27262

AMERICAN FOLK ART▪R
354 KENNESAW AVE.▪MARIETTA, GA. 30060

BACKWOODS FURNISHINGS▪M
ROUTE 28, BOX 161▪INDIAN LAKE, N.Y. 12842

BIELECKY BROTHERS▪R
306 E. 61ST. ST.▪NEW YORK, N.Y. 10021

ELLENBURG'S WICKER & CASUAL▪R
BOX 5628▪STATESVILLE, N.C. 28677

KELTER-MALCE▪R
361 BLEECKER ST.▪NEW YORK, N.Y. 10014

LODGEPOLE FURNITURE▪M
STAR ROUTE, BOX 15▪JACKSON, WYO. 83001

DANIEL MACK▪M
225 W. 106TH ST.▪NEW YORK, N.Y. 10025

POTCOVERS▪R
101 W. 28TH ST.▪NEW YORK, N.Y. 10001

JOHNNY TREMAIN SHOP▪R
COLONIAL INN▪MONUMENT ST.▪CONCORD, MASS. 01742

VANWORTH ANTIQUES▪R
23 STEVENS ST.▪LITTLETON, MASS. 01460

WALTERS WICKER WONDERLAND▪R
991 SECOND AVE.▪NEW YORK, N.Y. 10022

WILLOW & REED▪M
32–34 111TH ST.▪EAST ELMHURST, N.Y. 11369

THE WILLOW WORKS▪R
267 8TH ST.▪SAN FRANCISCO, CALIF. 94109

ZONA▪R
484 BROOME ST.▪NEW YORK, N.Y. 10013

PHOTO CREDITS

© Peter Aaron/Esto: 96, 138, 139, 146 × 2, 198–99, 234

Glen Allison: 92–93, 97, 102, 103 × 2, 121 × 2, 158, 202, 203 *lower*, 239

The Art Institute of Chicago, Mrs. Theodore Tieken Collection: 196

Baker Furniture Company: 176, 177

Benson Woodworking Company: 12–13

The Louis Bolduc House, Courtesy of the National Society of Colonial Dames, State of Missouri: 85, 174–75, 179

James Brett: 38, 39 × 2, 95 *lower left*

Karen Bussolini: 23, 28–32, 33 × 2 *left*, 36, 42, 46, 130, 206, 211, 231 *left*

Mario Carrieri, Courtesy of Knoll International: 165

Richard Collier, Courtesy of the Wyoming State Historical Society: 135

Derrick & Love: 43 × 2, 45

Ferenz Fedor, Courtesy of the Museum of New Mexico: 99

Jackie Foryst, Courtesy of Bader Binter: 230

John Fulker & Associates, Ltd.: 122, 123, 125 × 2

Gorham, Division of Textron: 162

Han Herr House, Lancaster, Pennsylvania: 69

Hickory Chair: 178 × 2

JSA Architects/Planners, James H. Somes, Jr.: 52

Lynn Karlin: 174 Reprinted by permission from *House Beautiful*. copyright January 1983. The Hearst Corporation. All rights reserved.

Lane Furniture Company: 184, 185, 186, 187

Robert Lautman: 106, 107, 108, 109

James Levin: 160–61, 163, 170, 208–9, 220 × 2, 221, 224, 225

Littlewood Communications: 169

Peter Loppacher: 56–57, 61, 62, 64, 65, 66, 67 × 2, 68. Photographs on pages 56–57, 66, and 67 appear courtesy of *House Beautiful's Building Manual*, copyright 1985, The Hearst Corporation.

The Manship House, Mississippi Department of Archives and History: 140, 228–29, 233

Norman McGrath: 58, 59, 90, 91, 118, 119 × 2, 147, 182–83, 188–89, 190–91, 192, 204, 205

The Metropolitan Museum of Art: 164, 166, 168

The Minnesota Historical Society: 193, 195 × 2, 197

The Mt. Vernon Ladies Association: 72, 73

The National Trust for Historic Preservation, "The Shadow": 70–71

The Nebraska State Historical Society, Butcher Collection: 22 *upper left*

The North Dakota Historical Society: 124

Kent Oppenheimer: 134, 150

Pearson, Clyde Pearson Company, A Division of Lane Furniture Company, American West Collection licensed by Museum of American Folk Art: 167

Robert Perron: 16, 17, 18, 19, 20, 21, 24 *lower right*, 25, 33 *lower right*, 37, 47, 48, 49 × 2, 50, 53, 63, 75, 76 × 2, 78, 84 × 2, 86, 88, 89, 95 *upper r t*, 104–5, 110, 143, 144–45, 148, 149, 154, 155, 156, 171, 172, 173, 180, 181, 210 × 2, 212, 213, 214, 215, 216, 217, 218, 219, 222, 223, 231 *lower right*, 235 × 2, 236, 237 × 2

Courtesy Ralph Lauren Home Collection 158–159

Bent Rej: 141, 142

Rejuvenation House Parts: 194

Murray Riss: 87

Edward C. Robinson III: 34, 35 × 2

Steve Rosenthal: 44, 54, 55, 136, 137 × 2

The Sagamore Lodge Conference Center: 64

Gordon Schenk, Jr.: 77, 79 × 2, 85, 100, 101 × 2

Sleepy Hollow Restorations: 66

Bill Stites: 82, 83

© Ezra Stoller/Esto: 81

Tim Street-Porter: 22 *lower*, 24 *left*, 94, 114–15, 120, 201, 203, *upper*, 227

Sam Sweezy: 8, 9, 11, 14–15

Timber Log Homes, Inc. of Marlborough, CT: 133 × 2

Timberpeg East, Inc./Lyman S. Perry/Architect: 40, 41

University of Chicago, Office of Special Events: 111, 112, 113

Joan Hix Vanderschuit: 126, 127, 128, 129

Venturi, Rauch & Scott Brown: 151, 152, 153

© Paul Warchol/Esto: 116, 117, 200

The Wisconsin State Historical Society: 132

INDEX